Narrative of a Journey From Tulpehocken, in Pennsylvania, to Onondago, the Headquarters of the Six Nations of Indians, Made in 1737 by Conrad Weiser

NARRATIVE

OF A

JOURNEY

FROM

TULPEHOCKEN, IN PENNSYLVANIA,

TO

ONONDAGO,

THE HEADQUARTERS OF THE SIX NATIONS OF INDIANS,

MADE IN 1737

BY

CONRAD WEISER.

————•◦•————

PHILADELPHIA,

JOHN PENNINGTON, No. 10 S FIFTH STREET.

COLLECTIONS

OF THE

HISTORICAL SOCIETY OF PENNSYLVANIA.

— — —

I.—*Copy of a Family Register in the handwriting of Conrad Weiser, now in the possession of Daniel Womelsdorf, of Womelsdorf, Berks County. Translated from the German by* HIESTER H. MUHLENBERG, M D , *of Reading, Pa*

In the year 1696, on the 2d November, I, Conrad Weiser, was born in Europe, in the land of Wirtemburg in the county (amt) of Herren-burg, the village is called Astacl, and was christened at Kupingen near by, as my father has informed me. I say, I was born on the second of November, sixteen hundred and ninety-six. My father's name was John Conrad Weiser, my mother's name was Anna Magdalena, her family name was Uebele. My grandfather was Jacob Weiser, my great grand-father also Jacob Weiser. He was magistrate (schultheiss) in the village of Great Astach, in the county (amt) of Backnang, also in the land of Wirtemburg. In this latter village my ancestors from time immemorial were born, and are buried there as well on my father's as my mother's side. In the year 1709, my mother passed into eternity on the last day of May, in the 43d year of her age, while pregnant with her sixteenth child, leaving children, Catrina, Margareta, Magdalena, Sabina, Conrad, George Frederick, Christopher, Barbara, John Frederick, and was buried there by the side of my ancestors. She was a woman fearing God, and much beloved by her neighbors. Her motto was, Jesus Christ I live for you, I die for you, thine am I in life and death

In the year above mentioned, namely in 1709, my father moved away from Great Astach on the 24th June. and took eight children with him. My eldest sister Catrina remained there with her husband, Conrad Boss, with whom she had two children. My father sold them his house, fields, meadows, vineyard and garden, but they could only pay him 75 gulden, the remainder 600 gulden was to be paid to my father at a subsequent period, which was never done, so it was made a present to them. In about two months we reached London in England, along with several thousand Germans whom Queen Ann, of glorious remembrance, had taken in charge, and was furnishing with food. About Christmas day we embarked, and ten ship loads with about 4000 souls were sent to America

The 13th June, 1710, we came to anchor at New York in North America, and in the same autumn were taken to Livingston's manor at the expense of the Queen   Here in Livingston's, or as it was called by the Germans Loewenstein's manor, we were to burn tar, and cultivate hemp, to repay the expenses incurred by the Queen in bringing us from Holland to England, and from England to New York. We were directed by several commissioners, viz., John Cast, Henry Meyer, Richard Seykott, who were put in authority over us by Robert Hunter, Governor of New York   But neither object succeeded, and in the year 1713 the people were discharged from their engagements and declared free.   Then the people scattered themselves over the whole province of New York. Many remained where they were   About 150 families determined to remove to Schochary,* (a place about forty English miles to the west of Albany) They therefore sent deputies to the land of the Maquas to consult with the Indians about it, who allowed them to occupy Schochary For the Indian deputies who were in England at the time the German people were lying in tents on the Blackmoor, had made a present to Queen Ann of this Schochary, that she might settle these people upon it   Indian guides were sent to show the Germans where Schochary was. My father was the first of the German deputies.

In November, 1713, when the above mentioned deputies had returned from the Maqua country to Livingston's manor, the people moved the same autumn to Albany and Schenectady, so as to be able to move in the spring to Schochary   Bread was very dear, but the people worked very hard for a living, and the old settlers were very kind and did much good to the Germans, although some of a different disposition were not wanting. My father reached Schenectady the same fall, where he remained with his family over winter with a man named John Meyndert

A chief of the Maqua nation named *Quaynant* visited my father, and they agreed that I should go with Quaynant into his country to learn the Maqua language   I accompanied him and reached the Maqua country in the latter end of November and lived with the Indians   here I suffered much from the excessive cold, for I was but badly clothed, and towards spring also from hunger, for the Indians had nothing to eat   A bushel of Indian corn was worth five to six shillings.   And at this period the Indians when drunk were so barbarous, that I was frequently obliged to hide from drunken Indians

1714.   In the spring my father removed from Schenectady to Schochary, with about 150 families in great poverty.   One borrowed a horse here, another there, also a cow and plow harness.   With these things they united and broke up jointly so much land, that they nearly raised enough corn for their own consumption the following year   But this year they suffered much from hunger, and made many meals on the wild potatoes and ground beans which grow in great abundance at that place.

* Scoharie

The Indians called the potatoes *Ochna-nada*, the ground beans *Otach-raguia*. When we wished for meal we had to travel 35 to 40 miles to get it, and had then to borrow it on credit. They would get a bushel of wheat here, a couple at another place, and were often absent from home three or four days before they could reach their suffering wives and children crying for bread.

The people had settled in villages, of which there were seven. The first and nearest, Schenectady, was called Kneskern-dorf,* 2d Gerlacho-dorf; 3d. Fuchsen-dorf, 4th Hans George Schmidts-dorf, 5th. Weisers-dorf, or Brunnen-dorf; 6th. Hartman's-dorf, 7th. Ober Weissers-dorf. So named after the deputies who were sent from Livingston's manor to the Maqua country.

Towards the end of July I returned from among the Indians to my father, and had made a considerable progress, or had learned the greater part of the Maqua language. An English mile from my father's house there lived several Maqua families, and there were always Maquas among us hunting, so that there was always something for me to do in interpreting, but without pay! There was no one else to be found among our people who understood the language, so that I gradually became completely master of the language, so far as my years and other circumstances permitted.

Here now this people lived peaceably for several years without preachers or magistrates. Each one did as he thought proper. About this time I became very sick and expected to die, and was willing to die, for my stepmother was indeed a stepmother to me. By her influence my father treated me very harshly; I had no other friend, and had to bear hunger and cold. I often thought of running away, but the sickness mentioned put a bit in my mouth, I was bound as if by a rope to remain with my father to obey him.

I have already mentioned that my father was a widower when he left Germany, and landed in 1710 with eight children, in New York, where my two brothers, George Frederick and Christopher were bound by the Governor, with my then sick father's consent, over to Long Island. The following winter my youngest brother, John Frederick, died in the sixth year of his age, and was buried in Livingston's *bush*, as the expression then was, and was the first one buried where now the Reformed Church in Weisers-dorf stands.

In the year 1711 my father married my stepmother, whom I have mentioned above. It was an unhappy match, and was the cause of my brothers and sisters' all becoming scattered. At last I was the only one left at home, except the three children he had by my stepmother, viz., John Frederick, Jacob, and Rebecca. Everything went crab-fashion, one misfortune after another happened to our family, of which I always was partaker. I frequently did not know where to turn, and learned to pray to God, and his word became my most agreeable reading.

But to return to Schochary. The people had taken possession without informing the Governor of New York, who after letting them know his dissatisfaction, sold the land to seven rich merchants, four of whom lived

* Dorf means village.

in Albany, the other three in New York. The names of those in Albany were Myndert Shyller, John Shyller, Robert Livingston, Peter Van Brugken; of those in New York were George Clerk, at that time Secretary, Doctor Stadts, Rip Van Dam. Upon this a great uproar arose both in Schochary and Albany, because many persons in Albany wished the poor people to retain their lands. The people of Schochary divided into two parties, the strongest did not wish to obey, but to keep the land, and therefore sent deputies to England to obtain a grant from George the first, not only for Schochary but for more land in addition. But the plans did not succeed according to their wishes, for in the first place the deputies had to leave secretly and embarked at Philadelphia in 1718. As soon as they got to sea they fell into the hands of pirates, who robbed them as well as the crew of their money, but then let them free.

My father, who was one of the deputies, was three times tied up and flogged, but would not confess to having money, finally, William Scheff, the other deputy, said to the pirates, this man and I have a purse in common, and I have already given it to you, he has nothing to give you, upon which they let him go free. The ship had to put into Boston to purchase necessaries for the crew and passengers, in place of those taken by the pirates. When they reached England they found times had changed, and that there was no longer a Queen Anne on the throne. They still found some of the old friends and advocates of the Germans, among whom were the Chaplains at the King's German Chapel, Messrs. Bohn and Roberts, who did all in their power. The affairs of the deputies finally reached the Lords Commissioners of Trade and Plantations, and the Governor of New York, Robert Hunter, was called home. In the meanwhile the deputies became in debt; Walrath, the third deputy, became homesick, and embarked on a vessel bound to New York, but died at sea. The other two were thrown into prison, they wrote in time for money, but, owing to the ignorance and over confidence of the persons who had the money to transmit which the people had collected, it reached England very slowly. In the meanwhile, Robert Hunter had arrived in England, had arranged the sale of the Schochary lands in his own way, before the Board of Trade and Plantations. The opposite party was in prison without friends or money. Finally, when a bill of exchange for seventy pounds sterling arrived, they were released from prison, petitioned anew, and in the end got an order to the newly arrived Governor of New York, William Burnet, to grant vacant land to the Germans who had been sent to New York by the deceased Queen Anne.

Towards the end of the year 1720, this William Burnet arrived in New York. In the commencement of the year 1721, I was sent to New York with a petition to Governor Burnet. He appeared friendly, and stated what kind of an order from the Lords of Trade and Plantations he brought with him, which he was resolved to comply with, but deputies were yet in England, not content with the decision, but could get nothing more done. In the last named year, viz., 1721, William Scheff returned home, having quarrelled with my father; they both had hard heads. At last, in the month of November, 1723, my father also returned. Scheff died six weeks after his return.

Governor Burnet gave patents for land to the few who were willing to settle in the Maqua country, namely, in Stony Arabia, and above the falls, but none on the river as the people hoped They therefore scattered, the larger part removed to the Maqua country or remained in Schochary, and bought the land from the before-named rich men.

The people got news of the land on *Suataro* and *Tulpehocken*, in Pennsylvania; many of them united and cut a road from Schochary to the Susquehanna river, carried their goods there, and made canoes, and floated down the river to the mouth of the Suataro creek, and drove their cattle over land. *This happened in the spring of the year* 1723. From there they came to Tulpehocken, and this was the origin of Tulpehocken settlement Others followed this party and settled there, at first also without the permission of the Proprietary of Pennsylvania or his Commissioners ; also against the consent of the Indians, from whom the land had not yet been purchased. There was no one among the people to govern them, each one did as he pleased, and their obstinacy has stood in their way ever since. Here I will leave them for a time, and describe my own circumstances.

In 1720, while my father was in England, I married my Ann Eva, and was given her in marriage, by the Reverend John Fredrick Heger, Reformed Clergyman, on the 22d of November, in my father's house in Schochary.

In 1722, the 7th of September, my son Philip was born, and was baptized by John Bernhart von Duhren, Lutheran clergyman ; his sponsors were Philip Brown and wife.

The 13th of January, 1725, my daughter Anna Madlina was born, was baptized by John Jacob Œhl, Reformed Clergyman, her sponsors were Christian Bouch, Junior, and my sister Barbara

In 1727, my daughter Maria was born on the 24th June, and was baptized by William Christopher Birkenmeyer, Luthern Clergyman. Her sponsors were Nicklas Feg and wife.

In 1728, December 24th, my son Frederick was born, was baptized by John Bernhart von Dilhren, Lutheran Clergyman ; his sponsors were Nicklas Feg and wife.

These four were born to me at Schochary. *Afterwards, namely, in* 1729, *I removed to Pennsylvania,* and settled in Tulpehocken, where the following children were born to me, namely :—

1730, the 27th February, my son Peter was born, and in 1731, the 15th February, I had two sons born, who were called Christopher and Jacob, the first lived 15 weeks, the latter 13 weeks, when they were released from the evils of this world and taken to a happy eternity.

1732, the 19th June, my daughter Elizabeth was born

1734, the 28th January, my daughter Margaret was born.

The 25th April, 1735, my son Samuel was born

The 18th July, 1736, I had again a son born to me. I called him Benjamin; when he was three months old, the care of the Almighty God took him away; the same year my daughter Elizabeth followed him. A

1*

merciful God will give them all to me again, to the honor of his happiness.

The 11th August, 1740, another son was born, I called his name Jabez. The mercy of God removed him from the evil of these days, when he was 17 days old.

The 27th of February, 1742, another daughter was born; I called her name Hanna, the following 11th August she went into a happy eternity.

The 16th of March of this year, my dear daughter Madlina, went from time to eternity, through an easy death, after a long and tedious illness. Her faith, consolation, and refuge was in the crucified Saviour, Jesus Christ, whom she had vowed herself to in days of health, with soul and body

The 12th August, Anno 1744, my son Benjamin was born

My father died July 13th, 1760

My mother went from time to eternity, on the 10th June, 1781.

———

II.—*Narrative of a journey, made in the year* 1737, *by Conrad Weiser, Indian Agent and Provincial Interpreter, from Tulpehocken* in the Province of Pennsylvania to Onondago, the head quarters of the allied Six Nations, in the province of New York. Translated from the German by* HIESTER H MUHLENBERG, M D., *of Reading, Pa*

In the year 1736, Governor Gooch, of Virginia, requested of the government in Philadelphia that it should make known to the so called Six Nations, by a regular embassy, that he, Gooch, was desirous of establishing a peace between the allied Six Nations living to the north, and the so called Cherokees and Cataubas to the South. And that he, Governor Gooch, had already so arranged, that the latter tribes would send deputies by next spring, to which place the chiefs of the allied Six Nations should also be invited; and in the mean time a truce should be proclaimed by them for a year long, to which the others had already agreed

I was required to perform this duty, and received regular instructions from James Logan, Esq., at that time President.

1737. On the 27th February, I left home for *Onontago*, which is the place where the allied Six Nations hold their council It is situated in the centre of these nations, on a river which empties into the great lake *Onontario*, from which the great St. Lawrence flows. I took with me as travelling companions Stoffel Stump, a white man, and an Onontager Indian who had been lying sick here since last summer, but had now recovered His name was *Ouis-yora*

———

* The Tulpehocken lands, comprising part of Berks and Lebanon counties, were settled in 1723, by Germans from Schohary, in New York, who penetrated the forests to the head waters of Susquehanna, where they built themselves canoes, and floated down the river to the mouth of the Swatara, on the head waters of which, and of the Tulpehocken, they settled, on lands which belonged to the Indians These lands were purchased by Thomas Penn of the Indians, in 1732 These were then the frontier settlements —H. H. M.

The 28th we remained at *Tolheo** on account of the bad weather, and to procure some necessaries for the journey

The 1st March we started from *Tolheo*, which is the last place in the inhabited part of Pennsylvania, and the same day we reached the top of the *Kulitunny* mountain   The snow was about a foot deep

The 2nd and 3d, we found nothing but ice under the new fallen snow on the north side of the mountain, which caused dangerous falls to ourselves and horses.

The 4th we reached *Shomoken*,† but did not find a living soul at home who could assist us in crossing the *Susquehanna* river.

The 5th we lay still, we had now made about eighty miles

The 6th we observed smoke on the other side of the river, about a mile above our camp; we went up opposite the place and saw a small hut. An Indian trader was induced by the repeated firing of our pieces to come over, who took us across safely in two trips, but not without great danger, on account of the smallness of the canoe, and the river being full of floating ice   We were here obliged to leave our horses behind, as it was impossible to get them across   We again lay still to day

The 7th, we started from here along one branch of the river.   The main stream comes from the north-east, we went to the north-west.   We found that we had commenced our journey at the wrong time; all the streams were filled with water and swollen, particularly those we had to cross   An old *Shanano*, by name *Jenomonona*, took us in his canoe across the creek at *Zilly-Squachne* ‡   I presented him with some needles and a pair of shoe strings, he was very thankful, and behaved as if he thought he had received a great present.

On the 8th we reached the village where *Shikelimo*§ lives, who was appointed by the President to be my companion and guide on the journey   He was, however, far from home on a hunt   The weather became bad and we lay by, the waters rose still higher, and no Indian could be induced to seek Shikelimo until

The 12th, when two young Indians agreed to go out in search of him   On the 16th they returned with word that Shikelimo would return by the next day, which so happened.   The waters had again risen by reason of the warm wind and rain, which melted the snow in the forests   Several Indians arrived by water from the Six Nations, who reported that the snow was still waist deep in the forests, and that it was not possible to proceed without snow shoes

* Tolheo was a gap in the Blue mountain, where the big Swatara breaks through, in Lebanon county, as stated in a letter from Conrad Weiser to Governor Morris, dated Oct 27, 1755, to be found in Rupp's History of Berks and Lebanon counties, page 41   There was subsequently a block house erected at this point, in the old French and Indian war of 1754, which was garrisoned by a company under Captain dusse, a part of the Penna battalion of nine companies under Lieut Col Weiser, raised for defence of the frontiers   This name Tolheo, has since degenerated into " *The Hole*,' as the *Hole* creek —H H. M.

† Now Sunbury —H H M

‡ Chishsquake creek.—H. H. M

§ This village I suppose to have been about Milton or near it. Shikelimo was the father of Logan, whose speech to Lord Dunmore on the murder of his family by Colonel Cresap is so well related in Jefferson's notes on Virginia.—H. H M.

The Indians at this place were out of provisions, our little stock was soon exhausted, as there was a numerous family in the house where we lodged. We had expected on leaving home to supply ourselves with provisions at this place, in which we were entirely disappointed   I saw a new blanket given for about one-third of a bushel of Indian corn   Here we began already to suffer the pangs of hunger, and other troubles forced themselves on us   It was with great difficulty that I procured a small quantity of corn meal and a few beans for the journey

The 21st we ventured to proceed on our journey to *Onontago*   There were now five of us, as Shikelimo acccompanied me, and we were joined by a warrior who had been on a war expedition to Virginia, and was going home in the same direction as we were travelling   In the forenoon we reached the large creek* *Canusorago*, it was very high; we were taken over in a canoe, not without great danger.   The next day two English traders attempted to cross, and their canoe was overturned by the the force of the current, one of them was drowned, and the other only escaped by swimming

To day we passed a place where the Indians in former times had a strong fortification† on a height, it was surrounded by a deep ditch, the earth was thrown up in the shape of a wall, about nine or ten feet high and as many broad.   But it is now in decay, as from appearance it had been deserted beyond the memory of man.

The 22d we came to a village called *Olstuago*, from a high rock which lies opposite   However, before we came in sight of the village, we reached a large creek‡ which looked more dreadful than the one of yesterday.   After repeated firing of our guns, two Indians came from the village to see what was to be done; they brought at our request a canoe from the village and took us across.   We quartered ourselves with Madame Montour, a French woman by birth, of a good family, but now in mode of life a complete Indian.   She treated us very well according to her means, but had very little to spare this time, or perhaps dared not let it be seen on the account of so many hungry Indians about   She several times in secret gave me and Stoffel as much as we could eat, which had not happened to us before for ten days; and showed great compassion for us, saying that none of the Indians where we were going had anything to eat, except the Onontagers, which my Indian fellow travellers refused to believe, until we found it true by experience.

The 23d we lay still on account of rainy weather   Two Indians arrived by water in a canoe made of elk skins, who said that in the high wilderness the snow was still knee deep   I received from Madame Montour some provisions for the journey   We have now advanced one hundred and thirty miles

The 24th we proceeded on our journey from here, and in the forenoon found the snow two feet deep, but as it had been very cold during the

* The Muncy creek?—H. H M.

† From the description this fortification appears to be of the same nature to those found in the Western States, showing that the builders of those great works also resided in Pennsylvania long previous as he remarks, it had been apparently at that early period, deserted long before.— H. H. M.

‡ The Loyalsock creek?—H. H. M.

previous night it was frozen so hard that we could walk over the surface without often breaking through the crust. In the afternoon we came to a thick forest where the snow was three feet deep, but not frozen so hard, which made our journey fatiguing. We were between two high and steep mountains, a small creek* flowed through the valley in an opposite direction to our course. The valley was not broader than the bed of the stream, and on both sides were frightful high mountains and rocks overgrown with carell or palm wood. The passage through here seemed to me altogether impossible, and I at once advised to turn back. The Indians, however, encouraged me to persevere, stating that in a little distance the mountains were further apart, and that we could easily proceed. I agreed at last to go on, the Indians took the lead, and clambered with hands and feet along the side of the mountain, we followed after. I had a small hatchet in my hand with which I broke the ice to give us foothold. There was considerable danger of freezing our feet, as we were often obliged to cross the stream and had no space to keep our feet warm by exercise. After clambering in this way we reached a point where the valley began to widen and become more spacious. We made a fire, and waited for our Onontager Indian who was far behind, because he was still weak from the illness he had undergone. In those three hours we had not advanced over one mile. The wood was altogether of the kind called by the English, Spruce, so thick that we could not generally see the sun shine. After we had warmed ourselves and taken some food, we proceeded onward, and in the evening made our camp under the Spruce trees. We broke branches to cover the snow where we lay down, and this constituted our beds. We made a large fire on the top of the snow which was three feet deep; in the morning the fire had burned down to the ground, and was as if in a deep hole. We slept soundly after our hard day's journey, but were all stiff in the morning from the cold, which during the night had been excessive. We prepared breakfast, which consisted of a little Indian corn and beans boiled in water.

The 25th, after breakfast, we proceeded on our journey, the snow was no deeper, and before noon we reached a stream which is a branch of the Otzmachson† river, which we had left yesterday. The stream we are now on, the Indians call *Diadachtu*‡ (the lost or bewildered,) which in fact deserves such a name. We proceeded along this stream between two terrible mountains, the valley was however now about a half mile in width, and the stream flowed now against this and then again against the other mountain, among the rocks. Here we held a long council as to the best mode of procedure, whether to remain in the valley and consequently be obliged to cross the stream repeatedly, or to endeavor to proceed along the sides of the mountains as we had done yesterday. As it was very cold to wade the creek often, we determined to try the mountain's side. As we were clambering along the mountains, before we had proceeded a quarter of a mile Shikelimo had an unlucky fall

* Quere, was it Trout run ?

† The West branch of Susquehanna. The orthography of these Indian names I find to vary in different portions of this journal, as if the writer were governed by the ear alone.

‡ The *Lycoming creek.*

which nearly cost him his life. He had caught hold of a flat stone, sticking in the root of a fallen tree, which came loose, and his feet slipping from under him, he fell at a place which was steeper than the roof of a house. He could not catch hold of anything, but continued slipping on the snow and ice for about three rods, when his pack, which he carried in Indian fashion with a strap round his breast, passed on one side of a sapling and he on the other, so that he remained hanging by the strap, until we could give him assistance. If he had slipped a half a rod further, he would have fallen over a precipice about 100 feet high upon other craggy rocks. I was two steps from him when he fell. We were all of us full of terror, but were obliged to proceed until we reached a place where we could descend into the valley, which did not take place for a quarter of an hour. When we reached the valley Shikellimo looked round at the height of the steep precipice on which he had fallen. We looked at him, he stood still in astonishment and said, *I thank the great Lord and Creator of the world that he had mercy on me, and wished me to continue to live longer*.

We soon came to the before mentioned water which had a strong current, we therefore cut a pole 12 or 15 feet long, of which we all took hold, and so waded together, in case that if any one should lose his footing, he could hold on to the pole. The water reached to the waist, but we crossed safely. We had to suffer from excessive cold, because the hard frozen snow was still 18 inches deep in the valley and prevented us from walking rapidly, neither could we warm ourselves by walking, because we had to cross the stream six or seven times. The wood was so thick, that for a mile at a time we could not find a place of the size of a hand, where the sunshine could penetrate, even in the clearest day. This night we prepared a place to sleep in the same manner as last night.

During the night it began to storm, and the wind blew terribly, which seemed to me strange. The Indians say that in this whole valley, which is about sixty miles long, it storms in this manner, or snows, every night. It is such a desolate region that I often thought I must perish in this frightful wilderness.

The 26th, we passed the whole day in travelling along the stream, the mountains continue high, and we were obliged to wade over the creek many times, but it began to diminish in size, so that we could cross it several times on fallen timber. To day *Tauwyerat* fell with such violence from one log on another, that he fainted and lay in that state for a considerable time. We became very much fatigued to day, from so often wading the creek in such cold weather, we also became very hungry; the provision was poor and little of that. This night we built a hut of branches, because it again became cloudy, it stormed again terribly and snowed at times as if it wished to bury us, but it never lasted long, and in the morning there was little snow on the ground.

The Indians believe that an *Othon*, (an evil spirit) has power in this valley, that some of them could call him by name and brought him sacrifices, by which he could be appeased. I asked if any of our party could do this, or knew his name They answered no, that but few could do this, and they were magicians

The 27th, we followed up the valley and creek, the hills became lower as we continued to ascend, because we had been following up this water from the time we left Madame Montour's. At noon we reached the summit of the mountain. Before we had quite reached the summit, we saw two sculls fixed on poles, the heads of men who had been killed there a long time before, by their prisoners, who had been taken in South Carolina The prisoners, who were two resolute men, had found themselves at night untied, which, without doubt, had been done by the *Otkon*, and having killed their captors and taken possession of their arms, had returned home.

One of the wonders* of nature is to be seen here. The creek already mentioned, is flowing as if on a summit or height of land , runs with a rapid current towards or against a linden tree, where it divides into two streams, the one stream becomes the water† up which we have been travelling for three days, and flowing to the *South* empties not far from the Indian village *Olstuaga*, into the *Quinachson*‡ river The other stream§ flows to the *North* and empties into the *Susquehanna* river, two hundred miles above *Shomoken* Both streams finally again unite their waters at Shomoken, where the *Otquinachson* river empties into the Susquehanna The stream flowing to the north, is called the Dawantaa, (the fretful or tedious.)

We travelled down this stream, and towards evening reached a place where the snow had entirely disappeared, in a grove of white oak trees. The south wind blew very warm, and the weather was pleasant, it seemed as if we had escaped from hell , we lay on the dry ground I cooked for supper as much as I thought would give us plenty to eat, as we hoped soon to reach the Susquehanna river where our Onontager had persuaded us that we would find provisions in plenty.

The 28th we eat our last meal for breakfast, as we believed that by evening at farthest we would reach the river, and started immediately after. The warm South wind was still blowing, and the sun shining. We left the *Dawantaa* to the right hand, and about ten o'clock reached a water called *Osrohu*,|| (the fierce) This is a rapid impetuous stream, because it flows among the mountains, and because the wind has melted the snow in the high forests. We first cut down a long pine tree, but it did not reach the other shore, and was carried away by the current The Indians advised that we should wade through, holding to a long pole, but I would not agree to that because the water was too deep. We knew not what to do , while we were cutting down the tree the water had risen a foot As we could not agree upon what was to be done, and were irrita-

* The beaver dam at the head waters of the Lycoming and Towanda Creeks, at the point where the lines of Bradford, Tioga, and Lycoming Counties meet. H H M
† The Lycoming Creek. H. H. M
‡ The West Brach of the Susquehanna H. H. M
§ The Towanda Creek H. H. M
|| This was *Sugar creek*, as he speaks afterwards of the Indians at the mouth of this creek feeding on the juice of sugar trees.—H. H. M.

ble from hunger, the Indians began to abuse Stoffel, who they said was to blame that I had not followed their advice. When I took his part they treated me the same way, called me a coward who loved his life, but must die of hunger on this spot I said it is true, we Europeans love our lives, but also those of our fellow creatures; the Indians on the contrary loved their lives also, but often murdered one another, which the Europeans did not do, and therefore the Indians were cruel creatures, whose advice could not be followed in circumstances like the present. They then wished to make a raft and thus cross to the other shore, which it was impossible to do at this place on the account of the rapidity of the current, and the rocks in the bed of the stream I said to them that I had so far followed their advice, but I now required them to follow mine, and to follow the stream downwards until we reached a quiet place, even if we had to go to the Susquehanna river, because on level land the water was not so rapid as among the hills and mountains Shikelimo answered that I did not know how far it was to the Susquehanna river, they knew it better than I did, it was an impossibility This he said to frighten me, but I knew it could not be more than a short day's journey by following the course we were travelling, because I examined the compass several times every day, I could also tell it by the mountains on the right hand side of the stream as we descended, which appeared to become lost, whereas up the stream they appeared much higher, from which a sound judgment would infer, that a man had not far to go to find the current lessen or cease. Shikelimo retorted that he was the guide, as being a person who had travelled the route often, while I had never done so, he would cross there, if I refused I must bear the blame if I lost my life by hunger or any other accident He would also complain to the Governor, Thomas Penn and James Logan, of my folly, and excuse himself The others spoke much to the same purpose, particularly *Tawagarat*, who was returning from the wars, who said openly, that he was too proud to obey a European I answered them all, and in particular Shikelimo; it is true, he was appointed by the Governor to be my guide, but not my commander, and since he would not guide me on the path I wished to go, namely, down the creek, and wished to be my master. I set him free from his duty, he might go where he pleased. I intended to be my own guide, and positively to take my own course with my fellow traveller Stoffel, but I would still advise him to obey me this time, which I did as a friendly request at parting. I then took my pack and moved off, the Onontager followed me immediately, Shikelimo did not hesitate long after he saw that I was in earnest, and soon followed. Tawagaret remained behind, because, as he said, he was too proud and obstinate to follow me We had gone more than a mile down stream, when I observed that nature had provided everything requisite for a safe crossing, the current had ceased entirely, and there was much dry pine timber, which is the lightest wood that can be found for such purposes Here I threw down my pack and ordered my companions to do the same. On their inquiring the reason, I said we would cross here. When Shikelimo observed the fine opportunity, he was glad, fired off his gun, and shouted to make our companion who remained behind hear We went to work, and in an hour and a half we had a raft

of the dry pine timber mentioned, ready, and passed over safely   Stoffel
and the Onontager crossed again to fetch two hatchets which we had forgotten, and all was done without any danger   We turned again up
stream until we struck our path.   My Indian companions thanked me for
my good council, and for resisting their wishes so boldly.   We travelled
rapidly for the purpose of reaching the Susquehanna river this evening,
where some Indians resided, and when we came in sight of it we sat down
to rest   yet we were in trouble for our obstinate *Tawagarat* who had remained behind.   After we had been sitting there for half an hour, we
heard a shout, and soon appeared Tawagarat at full speed but very wet.
On his questioning us as to how we had crossed, the Onontager related
the mode, at which he was surprised, and stated that he had tied several
pieces of wood together and pushed off into the water, but was so hurried
away by the current (in spite of his efforts with a pole) that he reached a
small island which was just above the place we crossed at, where the raft
separated, and he was obliged to wade the remaining distance with the
water up to his arm-pits.   I reproved him for his pride and obstinacy;
he acknowledged that he had acted foolishly, that he had heard our firing,
but was already engaged in making his raft.   We proceeded on our journey, well pleased that we were all together again, and the same evening
reached some Indians living on the Susquehanna river, where we, however, found nothing but hungry people, who sustained life with the juice
of the sugar trees   We, however, procured a little weak soup made of
corn meal.   I had a quantity of Indian trinkets with me, but could procure no meal   My only comfort this evening was, that whoever labors or
is tired will find sleep sweet.

The 29th we proceeded on our journey at an early hour, but without
breakfast, reached a dangerous place where the path on the bottom land
was overflowed by the river which was very high, and we had to cross
a very high mountain which was not much better than the one where
Shikehmo had met with his fall   We passed safely, and toward evening
we were also safely ferried in a canoe over the great branch of the Susquehanna river.   All the streams are very high, for the streams had been
uncommonly deep this winter.   This water is called * *Diu-ayon,* and
comes from the region of the *Siauhen* † and *Gaiuhers* ‡   There are
many Indians living here, partly Gaiuckers, partly *Mahikanders.*§
We went into several huts to get meat, but they had nothing, as they
said, for themselves   The men were mostly absent hunting, some of
the old mothers asked us for bread.   We returned to our quarters with a
Mahikander, who directed his old grey headed mother to cook a soup of
Indian corn.   She hung a large kettle of it over the fire, and also a smaller
one with potash, and made them both boil briskly.   What she was to do
with the potash was a mystery to me, for I soon saw that it was not for
the purpose of washing, as some of the Indians are in the practice of
doing, by making a lye, and washing their foul and dirty clothes.   For
the skin of her body   was not unlike the bark of a tree, from the dirt
which had not been washed off for a long time, and was quite dried in

*The Tioga river.—H H. M.   †Senecas —H H M.
‡Cayugas —H H. M   §Mohegans —H. H. M.

14

and cracked, and her finger nails were like eagles' claws. She finally took the ash kettle off the fire and put it aside until it had settled, and left a clear liquor on top, which she carefully poured into the kettle of corn. I enquired of my companions why this was done, and they told me it was the practice of these and the *Shawanos*, when they had neither meat nor grease, to mix their food with lye prepared in this manner, which made it slippery and pleasant to eat. When the soup was thus prepared,* the larger portion was given to us, and out of hunger I quietly eat a portion, which was not of a bad taste. The dirty cook and the unclean vessel were more repulsive. After I had eaten a little and quieted the worst cravings of hunger, I took some of my goods and quietly left the hut without being noticed by my companions, and went into another hut, gave the old grey headed mother 24 needles and six shoe strings, and begged her to give me some bread made of Indian corn, if it were only as much as I could eat at one meal. She immediately gave me five small loaves of about a pound weight, of which I and Stoffel eat two the same evening. The Indians eat so much of the soup that they became sick. We had intended to have had a day of rest here, if we could have procured meat, but had to be content to proceed on our journey.

The 30th we proceeded on our journey without any thing to eat except the remaining loaves, which were divided among us five. We passed a dangerous creek by wading in the shallow water, and passing the stream on a half fallen tree which hung across the water. The current was frightful. An Indian from the last village, who was to help us over the water, and show us the path, fell into the water so that we saw neither hide or hair, but soon rose and saved himself by swimming to the opposite shore to the one we were trying to reach. Towards evening we arrived at the branch *Oweyo*; the Indian village was on the other side of the river about a mile off. All the bottom land between us and the village was under water, and the current was rapid. We fired our guns three times, but no one would hear or show himself. If we had not seen the smoke of the huts, we would have thought the village was deserted. We began to prepare a fire and wood for a camp, and having made a long day's journey with hungry stomachs, were about to retire to sleep in that condition, and had already lain down, when a great storm came up from the west, with thunder and lightning, and such a violent rain that it was almost incredible. We could not find a place to lie down, but stood the whole night around the fire. Towards morning it became very cold, and ice formed in every direction, the day before having been very warm, and succeeded by the thunder storm of which it was the cause. At dawn we again commenced firing our pieces, on which a canoe with some women at last came from the village, to take us across the river, as we supposed. But they only came over the bottom land to the edge of the river, where they called to us that there were no men in the village, and the women could not venture to cross the raging flood; which was of so unusual a height, that bottom land was flooded, which had not been the case for many years, and in particular as their canoe was so small. *Tauayarat*,

*Quere, homony?

whose home was there, called to them to venture. When they heaid that it was Tawagarat they came across in safety, and stepped on shore; one of them spoke not a word, but wrapped her face in her blanket. The others gave the canoe to the Indians to ferry us across, and afterwards to bring the women. All which was done in three times crossing backwards and forwards, but not without great and imminent danger One paity was landed here, the othei there, in dry places, but still had to pass sundry hollows and ditches in water up to the breast, for the land is very uneven I went fiist in the canoe, four of us, of whom two Indians, went back with the canoe. I had new reasons to praise the protection of God, who had rescued us from such imminent peril; the water flew between the trees like arrows from a bow, where if we had struck one, of which theie were so many, we must have perished The Indians gladly received us into their huts, and showed us their compassion. Some of them were old acquaintances of mine from Schohary, they gave us food repeatedly, but each time only a little, so as not to injure our health They weie *Gauchers*. All the men were absent hunting, except a couple of old grey headed men, who had lodged at my house in Schohary some fifteen or sixteen years ago, and had shown me many favors accoiding to their ability. Tawagaiat remained here, and lodged in the hut ot his mothei-in-law; the woman who had hidden her face was his wife, and did so fiom modesty Such is the custom among the virtuous women of the Indian tribes. We remained here to-day to reciuit ouiselves a little, and also to procure provisions for the further progress of our jouiney

Apiil the 1st, we still iemained here, by my reckoning we are now 280 miles from home. •

April the 2nd, we started about noon on our journey and reached the water called *Onoto*, and were immediately taken across in a canoe. Several families of Onontagers live here, with one of whom, an old acquaintance, we took up oui lodgings, and weie well tieated.

The 3d we reached the village *Osteninhy*, inhabited by *Onontagers* and *Shavanos*. I was at this place in the year 1726, but hud my old acquaintances of that period partly absent, paitly dead. We had still five days journey accoiding, to the report of these Indians, fiom here to *Onontayo*, the object of oui tiresome journey, as we could not take the nearest route by ieason of the numeious cieeks, and must keep upon the hills. The family with whom we lodged had not a mouthful to eat. The larger part of this village had been living for more than a month on the juice of the sugar tree, which is as common here as hickory in Pennsylvania. We shared our small stock of provisions with sundry sick and children, who stood before us in teais while we were eating. Fiom the time we left Madame Montour's, I geneially gave to each one of us his daily portion; if I gave of my own poition a part to these poor creatures, I met with no sour looks, but if I took from the capital stock to give to them, my companions showed great disatisfaction But this did not hinder a thief fiom stealing, while we were asleep, the remainder of our stock of bread, which was but small. This was the first misfortune that happened to us, the second was, that we heaid the snow was still knee deep in the direction we were to travel, and that it was impossible to proceed, the third was, that the rainy weather in which we had arrived was turned to snow, of which eighteen inches fell in one night; the worst was that we had nothing to eat, and our bodily strength began to fail from many trials both of hunger and cold. Here we were obliged to remain and to pass the time in distress. I could, to be sure, purchase with needles and Indian shoe strings sugar made from the juice of the tree already mentioned, on which we sustained life, but it did not agree with us; we became quite ill from much drinking to quench the thirst caused by the sweetness of the sugar. My companion Stoffel became impatient and out of spirits, and wished himself dead. He desired me to procure a canoe in which to float down the streams until we reached Pennsylvania, which might have been done in six or eight days, but not without provisions and not without considerable danger, as the Susquehanna was very high and rapid, and we did not know the channel in such a swollen state of the water.

But I was now determined on no account to return home without accomplishing the object of my mission, in particular as I knew the danger of the river. Two weeks before I would gladly have turned back, as I foresaw all the difficulties we must undergo and conquer, but no one would then turn back, or see the difficulties I feared. Stoffel wished he had followed my advice at that time. I was now, however, so resigned to misery, that I could have submitted to the greatest bodily hardships without resistance, since I had been relieved from the tortures of the mind by the wonderful hand of God. I had at a previous period of my life wished that I had never heard of a God, either from my parents or other people, for the idea I had of him had led me away from him. I thought the atheists more happy than those who cared much about God. Oh, how far man is removed from God, yes inexpressibly far, although God is near, and cannot impart the least thing to corrupt man until he has given himself up without conditions, and in such a manner as cannot be explained or described, but may be experienced in great anguish of body and mind. How great is the mercy of the Lord and how frequent; his power, his goodness, and his truth are every where evident. In short our God created the heavens, the gods of the heathen are idols.

But to return to our affairs. I called the Indians together, represented to them the importance of my errand, stated what I was commanded to do by both the governments of Virginia and Pennsylvania, and required of them as faithful allies of the English, and particular friends of the government of Pennsylvania, to furnish me with provisions for my party so that I could reach Onontago, the end of my journey. Because the business related especially to the allied Six Nations, for whose sake their brother Thomas Penn had taken such an interest in the affair, and had sent me such a journey at an inclement time of year, for the purpose of preventing further bloodshed unnecessarily and out of mere revenge, and that they might possess their lands and raise their provisions in peace. In the next place I required them to send out two messengers on snow shoes as soon as possible, in advance, who should make known my approach, so that the councilmen of all Six Nations could be called together, which would require three weeks. There was an old war chief from

Onontago present, by whose interference both points were agreed to, only
no one knew where to procure provisions for us, or for the two Indian
messengers. By general consent a hut was broken into, whose occupants
were far absent on a hunt, and so much corn was taken as was judged
sufficient to enable us to reach Onontago. The two runners received a
share, and the balance, about one third of a bushel, was given to us, which
we thankfully received. I had it pounded at the house we occupied,
which was not done without loss. Hunger is a great tyrant, he does not
spare the best of friends, much less strangers. *Katoping*, a Frenchman,
who had been taken captive when a boy, but now an Indian in appearance, if not worse, together with another young Indian, were sent off to
notify my arrival to the council at Onontago. The last fall of snow was
rapidly disappearing as the weather had again become warm.

The 6th April the runners started. In the meanwhile an Indian had
the kindness to invite me privately to supper. I took Stoffel with me ;
he gave us to eat by night on two occasions. A third time, another old
acquaintance presented me with four small loaves one evening, which I
immediately divided among my companions and the surrounding hungry
children.

These Indians often came to my lodgings, or invited me to their huts
for the purpose of talking, (they are very inquisitive,) and thus we passed
the hungry hours away, in relating old or new events or traditions and
smoking tobacco, which they have in plenty. Among other things I
asked them how it happened that they were so short of provisions now,
while twelve years ago they had a greater supply than all the other
Indians; and now their children looked like dead persons and suffered
much from hunger. They answered that now game was scarce, and that
hunting had strangely failed since last winter; some of them had procured
nothing at all. That the Lord and Creator of the world was resolved to
destroy the Indians. One of their seers, whom they named, had seen a
vision of God, who had said to him the following words : *You inquire
after the cause why game has become scarce. I will tell you. You kill
it for the sake of the skins, which you give for strong liquor and drown
your senses, and kill one another, and carry on a dreadful debauchery.
Therefore have I driven the wild animals out of the country, for they
are mine. If you will do good and cease from your sins, I will bring
them back; if not, I will destroy you from off the earth* *

I inquired if they believed what the seer had seen and heard. They
answered, yes, some believed it would happen so, others also believed it,
but gave themselves no concern about it. Time will show, said they,
what is to happen to us, rum will kill us and leave the land clear for the
Europeans without strife or purchase.

The Indians living here are on an arm of the Susquehanna which
comes out of high mountains, and is a rapid stream. I saw the children
here walking up and down the banks of the stream along the low land,
where the high water had washed the wild potatoes or ground acorns out
of the ground. These grow here on a long stem or root about the size

* This remarkable language Weiser has put into his journal in large letters, by
way of calling attention to it.—H. H. M.

2*

of a thick straw, and there are frequently from five to ten hanging to such a root, which is often more than six feet long. The richer the soil, the longer they grow, and the greater the quantity in the ground. The largest are of the size of a pigeon's egg, or larger, and look much in size and shape like black acorns. I thought of the words of Job, chapter xxxi. 3—8, while these barbarians were satisfying their hunger with these roots, and rejoicing greatly when they found them in large numbers and dug them up.

On the 7th we agreed to leave this place at once, and again to pass through a great wilderness to reach the end of our journey. We started at 8 o'clock in the morning from this miserable place, where more murders occur than in any other nation. It is called by the Indians in particular a den of murderers, where every year so many are swallowed up. About noon we met our messengers returning, who said it was impossible to proceed on account of the deep snow in the mountains, which was more than knee deep. We debated long, and it was decided by a majority of voices to postpone the journey until better weather and roads. The before mentioned old war chief had accompanied us, because he was a leading man in the war council at Onontago, and wished to accompany me for the purpose of advancing my business to a favorable termination. He was a grey headed man of seventy years, as he showed by circumstantial proofs. He advised me confidently to proceed on the journey, and promised to guide us by such a route, that if we used our best efforts, we would by to-morrow evening reach a country where the snow had disappeared by reason of the open forests. After two days of fatigue and trouble, said he, you will be better off than by turning back with your business undone, after having already undergone so many hardships from cold, snow, high water, and hunger. I was pleased with his well meant advice, (for he often called me his son and child,) and bade him lead on; for he was much interested in the object of my mission. We proceeded on our journey, rainy weather set in, and before night we were in snow up to the knees. We made a hut this evening of the bark of the linden trees which we pealed off. It rained the whole night with a warm south wind which converted the snow into slush.

The 8th we travelled from early in the morning until evening with great rapidity, in constant rain, through a dreadful thick wilderness, such as I had never before seen. We frequently fell into holes and ditches, where we required the assistance of the others to extricate ourselves. We all lost courage. This was the hardest and most fatiguing day's journey I had ever made; my bodily strength was so exhausted that I trembled and shook so much all over, I thought I must fall from weariness and perish. I stepped aside, and sat down under a tree to die, which I hoped would be hastened by the cold approaching night. When my companions remarked my absence, they waited for me some time, then returned to seek me, and found me sitting under a tree. But I would not be persuaded to proceed, for I thought it beyond my power. The entreaties of the old chief and the sensible reasoning of Shikehmo (who said that evil days were better for us than good, for the first often warned us against sins and washed them out, while the latter often enticed us to sin) caused me alter my resolution, and I arose. But I could not keep up with the old man who was the leader and a good walker. He often waited for the whole party. We slept on the snow again that night, it rained the whole night, but not violently

The 9th, we prepared breakfast before day, and set out early in cloudy weather Before noon we got out of the thick forests into scattered groves where the snow had disappeared, as the old man had assured us. We seemed to have escaped out of all our troubles in this delightful region, especially as the sun broke through the clouds and cheered us with his warm rays. If the snow and the forests had remained the same as yesterday, we must all have perished before reaching Onontago But hunger was still pinching us; to eat a little corn meal soup was of no benefit, for it was only meal and water , the wheat bread and good meal had not only left the stomach, but the limbs also. We were now on high mountains, and to-day we passed the first waters flowing into the great lake *Onontario*, or the Saint Lawrence, out of which the famous river Saint Lawrence flows, which passes through New France or Canada. From all appearances this is the most elevated region in North America, we passed several small runs on the left hand, which join the lake just mentioned. To the right were others which joined the Susquehanna; a day's journey from here, there are waters emptying into the Hudson to the east, and to the west at some distance are the waters joining the *Meshasippia*. We reached several small lakes and ponds, at one of which the Indians said an evil spirit in the shape of a great snake resided, who was frequently visible. The Indians refused to drink here.

The 10th we left our camp quite early, as we hoped to reach the end of our journey this day. About noon we passed the hill on which, by Indian tradition, corn, pumpkins and tobacco first grew, and were discovered through an extraordinary vision. As we felt sure of reaching Onontago, we cooked the balance of our meal in a great hurry, and hastened onward. It began to rain hard. To-day we made forty miles, the timber was principally sugar trees. This evening we reached the first village of Onontago to our great delight. Not a soul remained in the houses, all came running out to see us ; they had been made acquainted with our coming by the old chief a quarter of an hour previously, who had preceded us for that purpose. They came in crowds to the house we occupied. I found here several acquaintances, but they were surprised at my miserable aspect ; one said it is he , another said no, it is another person altogether It is not the custom among these people, for a stranger who has come from a distance to speak until he is questioned, which is never done until he has had food set before him, and his clothes dried, in which things they did not allow us to want

Honor and praise, glory and power be given to the Almighty God who rescued us from so many and various evils and dangers, and saved us from death and destruction, from doubt and despair, and other hazards.

When on enquiry by the assembled males, I answered that I was sent to them by their brethren, *Onas* (Thomas Penn) and *James Logan*, with an extraordinary commission ; a messenger was immediately sent to the chief village, about four miles off, to make known my approach, and to ascertain the wishes of the council, whether I should remain here, or was to go forward At midnight the messenger returned, with advice that a house was prepared for me at the main village, where my arrival was anxiously awaited.

The 11th of April we were accompanied at an early hour to the village, and to the house which had been prepared for us, it was that of a man named *Annuar-oyon*, a relative of one of the chiefs, who received us kindly. After we had been left to ourselves, and had eaten something, the head man or chief came in, gave me a string of wampum according to the law and custom of their country, said I was very welcome on account of the message I was commissioned by brethren Onas and James Logan to deliver to their council That I could deliver it as soon I wished. I thanked them for their good will, and delivered a string of wampum in token of the greeting from their brethren Onas and James Logan, with a request that the whole council of the Six Nations might be called together as soon as possible. for the objects of the embassy I was sent on related to the whole of them, and were of great importance. They answered that of each nation, there were some chiefs present except of the *Caujuchos*, which need be no obstacle Those present were fully empowered to transact affairs of importance The following day was therefore appointed to give me an audience.

The 12th April they assembled at my lodgings to the number of about forty men, who all entered with great gravity and pride. When they were all collected to hear me, their *President* said to me that they were ready to hear me I arose and delivered my message in the *Maqua* language which I spoke with the most facility, and which they all understood. After each principal subject, of which there were two, I delivered to them a belt of wampum and a string of eight *klafter* long in the name of the Governor of Virginia, and Thomas Penn, proprietor of Pennsylvania They resolved to give me an answer in two days to the part relating to the truce, and to the congress at Williamsburg.

After all was over, a feast was prepared The food was brought in by other chiefs and set down in the middle of the house in a variety of vessels Each one brought his own dish and spoon, and helped himself to as much as he chose After the feast was over, the discourse turned on the events of our journey At a signal from the *speaker* they all went away, to allow us to retire to rest. I received in the evening already an intimation of the answer, which was full and satisfactory.

The 13th, Shikelimo was very sick, and also Stoffel, which was probably caused by imprudence in eating, but in two days they were again well

The 14th, the council again assembled, together with all the males who were at home, and the whole of my message was repeated by the *speaker*, and I was asked if it was correctly stated in all points. On my answering yes, the speaker proceeded, and their answer was given at large, with the remark that I should comprehend it fully, so as to be enabled to report it correctly to the Governor of Virginia and Onas They agreed to the truce, but decided against Williamsburg, and chose Albany as the place of the congress, all which can be seen in my English journal more at large, with all the speeches and incidents.

These Indians wished me to remain with them a month, until my strength should be restored, they showed every possible kindness to me, and we had no scarcity of food.

I became very sick, so that I expected to die, for half an hour I could neither hear nor see. My host gave me medicine after I had recovered my senses and could tell him to what cause I attributed this sudden attack; the medicine made a strong impression on my stomach and bowels, succeeded by a violent vomiting. After taking the medicine I was ordered to walk briskly until it operated, which took place in about half a mile from the village, where I lay until I became insensible. Towards evening I was found by several Indians, who led me home where a bed had been provided. At midnight I was well, other medicine was then given to me, and in the morning I arose perfectly restored, except that I felt weak.

I went with my host and another old friend to see a salt spring, of which there are great numbers, so that a person cannot drink of every stream on account of the salt water. The Indians boil handsome salt for use. These Indians, who are otherwise called *Onontagos* (people of the hills,) are the handsomest, wisest, and the bravest of the Six Nations. They live in huts made of bark, which are very convenient, some of them are 50, 60 to a 100 feet long, generally about 12 or 13 feet wide. In this length there are generally 4 to 5 fires and as many families, who are looked upon as one. The country is hilly, but there is a small valley which is very fertile, and yields almost incredible crops of corn, which is plentiful about here. The Europeans from Oswego, as well as Niagara, often come here for corn.

These Indians did all in their power to detain me longer, but I could not be content. I was tired of the Indian country and affairs. At my request they procured provisions for my return journey, and also a man to carry them and my pack.

On the 18th we took leave, (with my Stoffel and Shikelimo) for the purpose of returning home, if it should please the Supreme Being. The gods of the heathen are idols, the God of Israel created the heavens; he has a strong arm, but is patient, merciful, of great kindness, and is found by those who seek him. He is God.

This evening we reached the place where the Indians make bark canoes, on a creek passing by the village of Otsen-inky, of which we have already spoken. We peeled a chesnut tree and made a canoe. *Caxhayen*, who accompanied us, understood this work very completely. The weather set in bad, so that we had to lie by under a bark shelter. Snow fell a foot deep.

On the 22nd, we embarked in our newly made bark canoe, and pushed off; Caxhayen returned home. The first day we met many obstacles from fallen timber. This creek* is about the size of the *Tulpenpenhacken*. We had to unload the canoe several times to mend her. We crossed several lakes, and before night we reached a more rapid stream†

* Quere, was it Otsetic creek?   † Quere, was it Tiontoga creek?

which flowed among the hills with such rapidity as can hardly be described. We shot several ducks which are very plenty, and missed a deer and a bear

On the 23rd we reached deeper water, a river which comes from *Oneido*,[*] joins it at this point, the water was very high and rapid. *Saristaqua* of *Osten-inky* who was hunting, fired his gun on seeing us, and called to us. We turned to shore, which we reached in a few minutes, but had been carried down a mile since he had fired. He joined us, and I related what had taken place in Onontago, at which he was pleased. We left him, entered our canoe again, and by night reached Otsen-inky. Fired at a bear and missed

The 24th we pushed off early, in half an hour reached the Susquehanna river, passed to-day Onoto, Owego, down to the Dia-ogon. We found that at the last village we had forgotten our Onontago salt

The 25th we embarked early, got a companion, a relative of Shikeh-mo, but who was of little use, except to help us eat We passed the spot which we first reached after leaving the *desolate wilderness*, the mouth of Oshealui and Dawantaa Shot several ducks and a turkey. Passed several fine bodies of land, partly level, partly timbered

The 26th we reached *Scahanto-wano*,[†] where a number of Indians live, Shawanos and Mahickanders. Found there two traders from New York, and three men from the *Maqua* country who were hunting land; their names are Ludwig Rasselman, Martin Dillenbach, and Pit de Niger. Here[‡] there is a large body of land, the like of which is not to be found on the river

On the 27th we embarked; about noon we met some Pennsylvania traders, who gave us some rum.

On the 28th we reached Shomoken, here Shikelimo took leave of us and went home. Stoffel accompanied him, to bring the things we had left in his care, as saddles and bridles, and returned this evening on horseback. In the meanwhile I had paddled down the river on this side, to enquire after my horse of the Indians who were now encamped here. When I went on shore and looked into the forest, the first object I saw was my horse, about 20 rods off, and in fact not far from the spot where I had left him, when going up. Stoffel's horse could not be found at this time.

The 29th we set off over the country, on the 30th we reached *Tolhco*, and on the

1st day of May reached home in safety. Honor and praise, power and glory, be given to Almighty God for ever and ever.

[Here follows a German Hymn.—H. H. M.]

[*]Quere, was it Chenango river?   [†]Quere, the Lackawannoch river?
[‡]Quere. Wyoming valley?

III.—*Copy of a Journal of the proceedings of Conrad Weiser, in his journey to Ohio, with a message and present from the Government of Pennsylvania, to the Indians there.*

August the 11th, 1748. Set out from my house,* came to James Galbraith that day, 30 miles

The 12th, came to George Croghan's,† 15 miles.

The 13th, to Robert Dunning's, 20 miles.

The 14th, to *Tuscarora*‡ path, 30 miles.

The 15th, lay by on account of G Croghan's men coming back sick, and some other affairs hindering us.

The 17th, crossed Tuscarora hill; came to the Black Log lodging place, 20 miles

The 18th, had a great rain in the afternoon; came to within two miles of the Standing Stone, 21 miles

The 19th we travelled but 12 miles, and were obliged to dry our things

The 20th, came to Fraukstown, but saw no houses or cabins   Here we overtook one half of the goods,§ because 'four of George Croghan's men fell sick , 20 miles.

The 21st lay by, it rained all day

The 22nd, crossed *Allegeny*|| hills , came to the clear fields,¶ 16 miles.

The 23d, came to the Shawnee cabins, 34 miles

The 24th, found a dead man on the road who had killed himself by drinking too much whiskey. The place being very stony we could not dig a grave, and he smelled very strong, we laid him between two old logs, and covered him with stones and wood, and cut a great many saplings over him and went on our journey. Came to the 10 mile lake,** made 32 miles

The 25th, crossed *Kiskyminity* river , came to *Ohio* that day, 20 miles.

The 26th, hired a canoe, paid 1000 black wampum for the loan of it to Loystown , our horses being all tired we went by water, and came that night to a Delaware town , the Indians used us very kindly.

The 27th, set off again in the morning early by rainy weather. Dined

* Near Womelsdorf in Berks county —H. H M

† In Pennsboro, Cumberland County. Croghan was an Indian trader, who was to guide Weiser, and forward the goods.—H H M.

‡ The Tuscarora path seems to have led from the upper end of the Cumberland valley, probably from near Shippensburg to the Standing Stone, now the town of Huntingdon —H H. M

§ According to Gordon's History of Pennsylvania, page 257, goods to the value of one thousand pounds were sent as a present, and the instructions to Weiser are also given.—H. H M.

|| At Blair's gap, where the Indian path crossed the Allegheny mountain.—H. H M.

¶ Quere, the head waters of Clearfield creek, one of the head waters of the West Branch of the Susquehanna ?—H. H. M.

** Quere, Ten Mile Lick ?—H H. M.

24

in a Smicker town, where an old Smicker* woman reigns with great authority, in her house we dined, and they used us all very well. At this and the last mentioned Delaware town they received us by firing off a great many guns, especially at this last place. We had saluted the town by firing off four pair of pistols. Arrived that evening in Loystown,† we saluted the town as before, and the Indians fired above one hundredd guns, and great rejoicing appeared in their countenances. From the place where we took water, that is from the old Shawano's town, commonly called Chartierstown, to this place, it is above 60 miles by water, but about 35 or 40 by land.

The Indian council met this evening to shake hands with me, and to show their satisfaction at my safe arrival. I desired of them to send a couple of canoes to fetch down the goods from Chartier's old town, where we had been obliged to leave them because of our horses being all scalled on their backs, and tired   Gave them a string of wampum to enforce my request.

The 28th lay still.

The 29th, the Indians set off in three canoes to fetch the goods. I expected the goods would, by the time they could land at Chartier's old town, all have come from Frankstown, as we met about twenty horses of G. Croghan's at the Shawano cabins, in order to fetch them.

This day news came to the town, that the Six Nations were on the point of declaring war against the French, for the reason some of the French had imprisoned some of the Six Nations' chiefs who came to them as deputies   A council was held and all the Indians acquainted with the news, and it was said the Six Nations' message was by the way to give all the Indians notice to make ready to fight the French. That day my companions went to Caskasky, a large Indian town, about thirty miles off.

The 30th I went to Beaver creek, an Indian town about eight miles off, chiefly Delawares, the rest Mohocks, to have some belts of wampum made. This afternoon rainy weather set in which lasted about a week.   Andrew Montour came back from Caskasky with a message from the Indians there, to desire me the ensuing council might be held at their town.   We both lodged at this town at George Crogan's trading house

The 31st, sent Andrew back to *Caskasky* with a string of wampum, to let the Indians there know that it was an act of their own that the ensuing council must be held at Loystown; they had ordered it so last spring when George Croghan was up, and at the last treaty in Lancaster the *Shawanos* and *Twichtwees*‡ were told so, and they stayed accordingly for that purpose. Both would be offended if the council was to be held at Caskasky. Besides this, my instructions bind me to Loystown, and I could not go further without giving offence

September the 1st. The Indians at Loystown having heard of the message from Caskasky, called a council, and sent for me to know what I

* Queen Aliquippa —H. H. M.
† Loystown was about 12 or 14 miles below Pittsburg, on the right bank of the river —H. H. M.
‡ The Miami nation, I believe —H H M

was resolved to do, and told me the Indians at Caskasky were no more chiefs than themselves, and last spring they had nothing to eat, and expecting they would have nothing at my arrival ordered the council should be held here; now their corn is ripe they think to remove the council, but they ought to stand by their word, we have kept the Tweechwees here and our brethren the Shawanos from below on that account. I told them of the message I had sent by Andrew and they were content

The 2d the rain continued; the Indians brought us a good deal of venison

The 3d Set up the Union flag on a long pole; treated all the company with a dram of rum The king's health was drunk by Indians and white men Towards night a great many Indians arrived to attend the council. There was great firing on both sides. The strangers first saluted the town at 'about a quarter of a mile distance, and at their entry the town people fired furiously, also the English traders, there were about twenty of them At night I was taken sick with the colic, got bled

The 4th was obliged to keep my bed all day, and was very weak.

The 5th I found myself better *Scayhuhady* came to see me; had some discourse with him about the ensuing council.

The 6th, one canoe with goods arrived, the rest did not come to the river. The Indians that brought the goods found our casks of whiskey hid by some of the traders, they had drunk two and brought two to the town The Indians all got drunk to night, and some of the traders along with them The weather cleared up

The 7th being informed the *Wantats* had a mind to go back again to the French, and had endeavored to take the Delawares along with them to recommend them to the French, I sent Andrew to Beaver Creek with a string of wampum to inform himself of the truth of the matter. They sent a string in answer to let me know they had no correspondence that way with the Wantats, and the aforesaid report was false

The 8th had a council with the chiefs of the Wantats, inquired their number, and what made them come away from the French, what correspondence they had with the Six Nations, and whether or no they ever had any correspondence with the Governor of New York They informed me that their coming away from the French was owing to the hard usage they received from them, they would always get their young people to go to war against their (the French) enemies, and would use them as their own people, that is, like slaves, and their goods were so dear, they (the Indians) could not buy them That there were one hundred fighting men came over the lakes to the English; seventy were left behind at another town a good distance off They hoped they would follow them That they had a very good correspondence with the Six Nations these many years, and are one people with them, that they could wish the Six Nations would act more briskly against the French. That above fifty years ago they made a treaty of friendship with the Governor of New York at Albany. They showed a large belt of wampum they received then by the said Governor as from the King of Great Britain The belt was 25 grains wide and 265 long, very curiously wrought; there were seven images of men holding one another by the hand, the first signifying the Governor of New York, (or rather as they said the King of Great Britain,) the second the Mohacks, the third the Oneiders, the fourth the Cayuckers, the fifth the Onontagers, the sixth the Sinickers, the seventh the Wantats, and two rows of black wampum under their feet through the whole length of the belt, to signify the road from Albany through the five nations to the Wantats. That six years ago they had sent deputies to Albany with the same belt to renew the friendship

I treated them with a quart of whiskey and a roll of tobacco They signified their good wishes to King George and all his people, and were mightily pleased that I looked upon them as brethren of the English.

This day I desired the deputies of all the nations of Indians on the waters of the Ohio to give me a list of all their fighting men, which they promised to do.

A great many of the Indians went away to-day because the rest of the goods did not come, and the people in this town could not find provision enough, the number was too great.

The following is the number of every nation's fighting men, given to me by their several deputies in council in so many little sticks tied up in a bundle

The Sinickers,			·	·	·	163
" Shawanos,	·		·	·	·	162
" Wantats,	·	·		·	·	100
" Zisagechroanu,	·		·	·	·	40
" Mohacks, (among whom are 27 French Mohacks,)					·	74
" Mahickans,	·	·	·		·	15
" Onontagers	·	·		·	·	35
" Cayuckers,	·	·		·	·	20
" Oneiders,			·	·	·	15
" Delawares,		·	·	·	·	165

Total, 789

The 9th, I had a council with the Sinickers, gave them a large string of wampum, black and white, to let them know that I had a charge from the President and Council in Philadelphia, to make inquiry who took the people prisoners, lately taken in Carolina, one thereof being a great man, and that by what discovery I had already made, I had found it was some of the Sinickers did it I therefore desired them to give me their reason for so doing; and, as they had struck their hatchet into their brethren's body, they could not expect that I could deliver my message with a good heart before they gave me satisfaction in that respect For they must consider the English, though living in several provinces, are all one people, and doing mischief to one is doing mischief to the other Let me have a direct and plain answer.

The 10th, a great many of the Indians got drunk; one Henry Nolling had brought near thirty gallons of whiskey to the town This day I made a present to the old Shawano chief, *Cachkauatchiky*, of a stroud watchcoat, a blanket, a common matchcoat, a shirt, a pair of stockings, and a large twist of tobacco. I told him the President and Council at Philadelphia remembered their old and true friend, and would clothe his old body once more, and wished that he might wear out these clothes, and live so much longer, as to give them an opportunity to clothe him again. There were a great many of the Shawano Indians present; among others, the Big Huming and the Bride, being two of them that went off with Peter Chartier, but protested against our traders. Caekcawatchiky returned many thanks, and some of the Six Nations did the same, and expressed their satisfaction to see that a true man was taken notice of, although he was now grown childish

The 11th, I staved, in concert with George Croghan, an eight gallon cask of whiskey, belonging to the aforesaid Henry Nolling, who could not be prevailed upon to hide it in the woods, but would sell it and drink himself.

I desired the Indians in council to send some of their young men to meet our people with the goods, and not come back until they heard of or saw them. I begun to be afraid they had fallen into the hands of the enemy, so did the Indians themselves. Ten warriors from *Niagara* came to town by water. We suspected them very much, and feared that some of their parties went to meet our people, by hearing of them coming down the river.

The 12th, two Indians and Robert Callender, went out to meet our people with the goods; had orders not to come back before they saw them, or to go to Frankstown where we left the goods

The same day the Indians made answer to my request concerning the prisoners taken in Carolina *Thanayieson*, a Sineker, spoke to the following purport, out of doors, in the presence of all the deputies of the other nations. The speaker directed his discourse to the English in general, had a string of wampum in his hand, and said, Brethren, you came a great way to visit us, and many sorts of evil might have befallen you by the way, which might have been hurtful to your eyes and your inward parts, for the woods are full of evil spirits. We give you this string of wampum to clear up your eyes and minds, and to remove all bitterness of your spirits, that you may hear us speak in good cheer. Then the speaker took the belt of wampum in his hands and said, Brethren, when we and you first saw one another at your first arrival at Albany, we shook hands together, and we became brethren, and we tied your ship to the bushes, and after having had more acquaintance with you we loved you more and more, and perceiving a bush would not hold your ship, we then tied it to a big tree, and ever since good friendship continued between us. Afterwards, you, our Brethren, told us a tree may happen to fall down and the rope rot wherewith the ship was tied; you then proposed to make a silver chain, and tie your ship to the great mountain in the Five Nation's country, and that chain was called the chain of friendship We were all tied by our arms together with it, and we, the Indians of the Five Nations, heartily agreed to it, and ever since a very good correspondence has been kept between us; but we are very sorry that, at your coming here, we are obliged to talk of the accident that lately befell you in Carolina, where some of our warriors, by the instigation of the Evil Spirit, struck their hatchet into our own body, for our brethren, the English, and we, are of one body, and what was done we utterly abhor as a thing done by the Evil Spirit himself. We never expected any of our people would do so to our brethren, we therefore remove our hatchet, which by the Evil Spirit's order was struck into your body, and we desire that our brethren, the Governor of New York, and Onas,* may use their utmost endeavors that the thing may be buried into the bottomless pit, that it may never be seen again, that the chain of friendship, which is of so long standing, may be preserved bright and unhurt (Gave the belt.)

Then the speaker took up a string of wampum, mostly all black, and said, Brethren, as we have removed our hatchet out of your body, or, properly speaking, out of our own, we now desire that the air may be cleared up again, and the wound given may be healed, and every thing put in a good understanding, as it was before, and we desire you will assist us to make up every thing with the Governor of Carolina The man that has been taken prisoner we now deliver up to you, he is yours (Laid down the string and took the prisoner by the hand and delivered him into my hand.)

By the way of discourse, the speaker said that the Six Nation warriors often met Englishmen trading to the Catawbas, and often found that the English betrayed them to their enemy, and some of the English traders had been spoken to by the said speaker last year in the Cherokees country, and told them not to do so. That the speaker and many others of the Six Nations had been afraid a long time, that such a thing by some of their warriors at one time or another would be done

The same day had a council with the Smickers and the Onontagers about the Wantats, to receive them into our union. I gave a large belt of wampum, and the Indians gave two, and every thing was agreed upon that should be said to the Wantats. The same evening a full council was appointed and met accordingly. A speech was made to the Wantats as follows, by *Asserhaihu*, a Smicker. Brethren, the Jonontaty Hages, last spring you sent this belt of wampum to us (having the belt then in his hands,) to desire us and our brethren, the Shawanos, and our cousins the Delawares, to come and meet you in your retreat from the French, and we accordingly came to your assistance and brought you here, and we received you as our own flesh. We desire you will think you are now joined to us and our brethren, the English, and you are become one people with us; then he laid that belt by, and gave them a very large string of wampum. The speaker took up the belt and said, Brethren, the English our brethren, bid you welcome, and are glad you escaped out of captivity; you have been kept as slaves by Onontio,† notwithstanding he called you all along his children, but now you have broke the rope wherewith you have been tied and become freemen, and we, the United Six Nations, receive you to our council fire, and make you members thereof, and we will secure your dwelling place to you against all manner of danger. (Gave the belt)

* Penn, or the Government of Pennsylvania
† The French.

Brethren we the united nations and all our Indian allies, with our brethren the English, look upon you as our children, though you are our
brethren; we desire you will give no ear to the Evil Spirit that spreads
lies and wickedness. Let your mind be easy and clean, and be of the same
mind with us, whatever you may hear: nothing shall befall you but what
of necessity must befall us in the same time   (Gave the belt.)

Brethren, we the Six united Nations and all our Indian allies, with
our brethren the English, are extremely glad to see you here, as it happened just at the same time when our brother Onas is with us, we jointly by this belt of wampum embrace you about your middle, and desire
you to be strong in your mind and heart; let nothing alter your mind
but live and die with us.   (Gave the belt and the council broke up.)

The 14th, a full council was summoned, and every thing was repeated
by me to all the Indians, that had passed in Lancaster at the last treaty
with the Twichwees

The news was confirmed by a belt of wampum from the Six Nations,
that the French had imprisoned some of the Six Nations' Deputies, and
thirty of the Wantats, including women and children.

The Indians that were sent to meet our people with the goods, came
back and did not see any thing of them, but they had been no further
than the Shawanos' old town

The 15th, I let the Indians know that I would deliver my message to
morrow, and the goods I had, and they must send deputies to me on my
returning homewards, and wheresoever we should meet the rest of the
goods I would deliver them to them, if they are not taken by the enemy,
to which they agreed

The same day the Delawares made a speech to me, and presented a beaver coat and a string of wampum and said, Brother, we let the President
and Council of Philadelphia know, that after the death of our chief man,
Olumapies, our grand children the Shawanoes came to our town in order
to condole with us over the loss of our good King, your brother, and
they wiped off our tears and comforted our minds, and as the Delawares
are the same people with the Pennsylvanians, and born in one and the
same country, we give some of the present our grand children gave us, to
the President and council in Philadelphia, because the death of their
good friend and brother must have effected these as well as us   (Gave
the beaver coat and a string of wampum.)

The same day, the Wantats sent for me and Andrew, and presented
us with seven beaver skins, about ten pounds weight and said, they gave us
that to buy some refreshment for us after our arrival in Pennsylvania,
wished that we might get home safe, and lifted up their hands and said
that they would pray God to protect us and guide us the way home   I
desired to know all their names they withal behaved in every respect
like people of great sense and sincerity, for the most part were grey
headed men; their names are as follows —Totornihiadases, Taganayiosy,
Sonachqua, Wanduny, Taruchiorus their speaker. The chiefs of the
Delawares that made the above speech are Shawanapon and Achaman-
tama

I now made answer to the Delawares and said, Brethren, the Dela-

3'

wares, it is true what you said, that the people of Pennsylvania are your brethren and countrymen, we are very well pleased at what your childdren the Shawanos did to you. This is the first time we had public notice given us of the death of our good friend Olumapies. I take this opportunity to remove the remainder of trouble from your hearts, to enable you to attend in council at the ensuing treaty, and I assure you the President and council of Pennsylvania condole with you over the loss of your king, our good friend and brother (Gave five strouds.)

The two aforesaid chiefs gave a string of wampum, and desired me to let their brethren the President and council know they intended a journey next spring to Philadelphia, to consult with their brethren over some affairs of moment Since they are now like orphan children, they hoped their brethren would let them have their good advice and assistance, as the people of Pennsylvania and the Delawares were like one family

The same day the rest of the goods arrived The men informed me that they had ten days rain, and the creeks rose, and that they had been obliged to send one sick man back from Frankstown to the inhabitants, with another that attended him.

The neighboring Indians being sent for again, the council was appointed to meet to-morrow. It rained again

The 17th it rained very hard, but in the afternoon it held up for about three hours, the Deputies of the several nations met in council, and I delivered to them what I had to say from the President and council of Philadelphia.

Brethren, you that live off in Ohio, I am sent to you by the President and council of Pennsylvania, and I am now going to speak to you on their Honors' behalf. I desire you will take notice and hear what I shall say (Gave a string of wampum.)

Brethren, some of you were in Philadelphia last fall, and acquainted us that you had taken up the English hatchet, and that you had already made use of it against the French, and that the Frenchmen had very hard heads, and your country afforded nothing but grass and sticks, which were not sufficient to break them. You desired your brethren would assist you with some weapons sufficient to do it, your brethren the President and council promised you then to send something to you next spring by *Tharachauayon*, but as some other affairs prevented his journey to Ohio, you received a supply by George Croghan, sent to you by your brethren. But before George Croghan came back from Ohio, news came from over the great lake that the King of Great Britain and the French King had agreed upon cessasion of arms for six months, and that a peace was very likely to follow it Your brethren, the President and council, were then in a manner at a loss what to do; it did not become them to act contrary to the command of the King, and to war against the French, but as your brethren never missed in fulfilling their promises, they have on a second consideration thought proper to turn their intended supply into a civil and brotherly present, and have accordingly sent me with it, and here are the goods before your eyes, which I have by your brethren's order divided into five shares, and laid into five different heaps, one heap thereof your brother Assaryquoh* sent to you to remember his friendship and unity with you, and as you are all of the same nation with whom we English have been in league of friendship, nothing need to be said more than only this, that it is a present from your brethren the President and council and Assaryquoh, and shall serve to strengthen the chain of friendship between us, the English, and the several nations of Indians to which you belong. A French peace is a very uncertain one, they keep it no longer than their interest permits, then they break it without provocation given them. The French King's people have been almost starved in old France for want of provision, that made them wish and seek for peace, but our wise people are of opinion that after their belly is full, they will quarrel again and raise a war All the nations in Europe know that their friendship is mixed with poison, and many that trusted too much on their friendship, have been ruined. I now conclude and say that we the English are your true brethren at all events, in token whereof, receive this present.

The goods being then uncovered, I proceeded, "Brethren, you have of late settled the river of Ohio for the sake of hunting, and our traders followed you for the sake of hunting also, you have invited them yourselves Your brethren, the President and council, desire you will look upon them as your brethren, and see that they have justice done. Some of your young men have robbed the traders, but you will be so honest as to compel them to make satisfaction You are now become a people of note, and grow very numerous of late years, and there are without doubt some wise men among you It becomes you to act the part of wise people and be more regular than you have been for some years, when only a few young hunters lived here.

(Gave a belt)

Brethren you have of late made frequent complaints against the traders for bringing so much rum into your towns, and you desired it might be stopped, and your brethren the President and council made an act accordingly, and put a stop to it, and no trader was to bring any rum or strong liquor into your towns. I have the act here with me, and shall explain it to you before I leave you, but it seems it is out of your power to stop it entirely You send down your own skins by the traders to buy rum for you, you go yourselves down and fetch horse loads of strong liquor. But the other day, an Indian came from this town out of Maryland with three horse loads of liquor, so that it appears that you love it so well that you cannot be without it. You know very well, too, that the country near the Endless mountain affords strong liquor, and the minute the traders buy it they are gone out of the inhabitants and are travelling to this place without being discovered Besides this, you never agree about it; one will have, the others won't have it, (though very few of them) a third says we will have it cheaper This last we believe speaks out of your heart, (here they laughed) Your brethren, therefore, have ordered that every cask of whiskey shall be sold to you for five books† in your towns, and if the traders offer to sell whiskey to you and will not let you have it at that price, you may take it from them and drink it for nothing.

* Who is intended ? H. H. M.
† Quere, Buckskins ?

(Gave a belt.)

Brethren, here is one of the traders whom you know to be a very sober and honest man, he has been robbed out of the value of 300 books, and you all know by whom   Let therefore satisfaction be made to the trader

(Gave a string of wampum)

Brethren I have no more to say."

I delivered the goods to them having divided them before into five shares, gave a share to the Sinkers, a share to Kayuckers, Onontagers, Oneiders, and Mohacks, the third share to the Delawares, the fourth to the Wantats, Zisagechroanu, and Mahiekans, the fifth to the Shawnoes

The Indians signified great satisfaction and joy, and were well pleased with the cessation of arms; the rainy weather hastened them away with the goods into some houses, and night coming on, the speech was delivered to the Delawares in their own language by Andrew Montour, in my presence and some of the traders

I acquainted the Indians I was resolved to leave them to-morrow and return homewards

The 19th *Scahuhady, Tanughrishon,* and *Oniadagai chra,* with a few more, came to my lodging and spoke to the following purport

Brother Onas, we desire you will hear what we are going to say to you in behalf of all the Indians on the Ohio. Their deputies have sent us to you, we have heard what you have said to us and we return you many thanks for the kindness in informing us of what passed between the king of Great Britain and the French King   In particular, we return you many thanks for the large presents, the same we do to our brother Assariquoh who joined our brother Onas in making us a present   Our brethren have indeed tied our hearts to theirs; we at present can but return thanks with an empty hand till another opportunity serves   To do it sufficiently we must call a great council and do everything regular, in the meantime look upon us as your true brethren.

Brother, you said the other day in council, if anything befell us from the French we must let you know of it; we will let you know if we hear anything from the French, be it against us or yourselves. You will have peace, but it is most certain that the Six Nations and their allies are upon the point of making war against the French. Let us keep up a true correspondence, and let us hear always of one another

(They gave a belt.)

Scahuhady and the half king with two others had informed me that they often must send messengers to Indian towns and nations, and had nothing in their council bag (as they being beggars) either to recompense a messenger or to get wampum to do their business, and begged I would assist them with something. I had saved a piece of strouds and a half barrel of powder, one hundred pounds of lead, ten shirts, six knives, one pound of vermillion, and gave it to them now for the aforesaid use. They returned many thanks and were mightily pleased.

The old Sinicker Queen from above, already mentioned, came to inform me some time ago that she had sent a string of wampum of three fathoms to Philadelphia by James Dunnings, to desire her brethren would send her up a cask of powder and some small shot to enable her to send out the Indian boys to kill turkeys and other fowls for her, whilst the men are gone to war against the French, that they may not be starved I told her I had heard nothing of her message, but if she had told me of it before I had parted with all the powder and lead, I could have let her have some, and promised I would make inquiry ; perhaps her messenger had lost it on the way to Philadelphia I gave her a shirt, a Dutch wooden pipe and some tobacco. She seemed to have taken a little affront because I took not sufficient notice of her in coming down I told her she acted very imprudently not to let me know by some of her friends who she was, as she knew very well I could not know by myself She was satisfied, and went away with a deal of kind expressions

The same day I gave a stroud, a shirt and a pair of stockings to the young Shawano, King Capechque, and a pipe and some tobacco.

The same day, about 12 o'clock, we set out for Pennsylvania, and travelled about twelve miles ; rainy weather.

The 20th, left a horse behind that we could not find. Came to the river, had a great rain ; the river not rideable.

The 21st, sent for a canoe about 6 miles up the river to a Delaware town An Indian brought one, we paid him a blanket, got over the river about 12 o'clock. Crossed Kiskanmnity creek, and came that night to the round hole, about twelve miles from the river.

The 22d, the weather cleared up ; we travelled this day about 35 miles, came by the place where we had buried the body of John Quen, but found the bears had pulled him out and left nothing of him but a few naked bones and some old rags.

The 23rd, crossed the head of the West Branch of the Susquehanna, about noon come to the Cheasts. This night we had a great frost, our kettle standing about four or five feet from the fire, was frozen over with ice thicker than a brass penny.

The 24th, got over Allegheny hill, otherwise called mountains, to Frankstown, about 20 miles.

The 25th, came to the Standing Stone ; slept three miles at this side, about 31 miles.

The 26th, to the forks of the wood about 30 miles ; left my man's horse behind as he was tired

The 27th it rained very fast ; travelled in the rain all day ; came about 25 miles.

The 28th, rain continued, came to a place where white people now begin to settle, and arrived at George Croghan's in Pennsbury, about an hour after dark, came about 35 miles that day, but we left our baggage behind

The 29th and 30th, I rested myself at George Croghan's, in the mean time our baggage was sent for, which arrived

The 1st of October reached the heads of Tulpenhocken.

The 2nd I arrived safe at my house

IV.—*Letter from Mr Rembrandt Peale to a Member of the Historical Society of Pennsylvania, on the First Experiments of Fitch and Fulton in Steam Navigation.*

PHILADELPHIA, JAN. 13th, 1848

Dear Sir,—I cheerfully comply with your request to commit to paper some incidents of which I live to bear testimony, in relation to the origin of Steam Navigation. I do this the more readily, because *Romance* too often usurps the place of *History*, and disguises every branch of knowledge, as I know it does my own particular Art; there being many persons who take little interest in its history unless they are excited by the most marvellous anecdotes of painters I leave to others the investigation of the first *conception* of Steam Navigation —*the Chronology of the idea*—and shall merely relate the events of which I was an eye-witness; with the conclusions which must be drawn from them.

In the spring of 1785, hearing there was something curious to be seen at the floating bridge on the Schuykill at Market Street, I eagerly ran to the spot, where I found a few persons collected, anxiously gazing at a shallop at anchor below the bridge, with about 20 persons on board. On the deck was a small furnace, and machinery connected with a complex crank, projecting over the stern, to give motion to three or four paddles, resembling snow shovels, which hung into the water. When all was ready, and the force of steam was made to act, by means of which I was then ignorant, knowing nothing of the nature of a piston except in the common pump, the paddles began to work, pressing against the water *backwards* as they rose, and the boat, to my great delight, moved against the tide, without wind or hand, but in a few minutes it ran aground at an angle of the river, owing to the difficulty of managing the unwieldly rudder which projected eight or ten feet It was soon backed off and proceeded slowly to its destination at Gray's ferry. So far it must have been satisfactory to Mr. FITCH, in this his first public experiment. I was not in the way of hearing anything of his views, but understood that soon afterwards he repeated his experiment on the Delaware, with improved paddles at the sides of the vessel; which is incorrectly recorded as his *first* experiment It induced several gentlemen to furnish him with the means of going to England for the purpose of prosecuting his invention—but he died on the voyage. It is known that Mr FULTON was a fellow passenger, and there is every reason to suppose that they freely conferred on the subject of Steam Navigation, being both men of frank and liberal minds. Mr. Fulton's motive in going to England was to cultivate his talent for painting, and to place himself, as he did, with Mr. WEST, who spoke to me of his character in the highest terms. Although he was successful in a great degree, of which his works bear evidence, yet he feared that America might not afford sufficient encouragement in the fine arts He therefore decided to visit Paris, and devote his studies to civil engineering, as affording a better field for enterprise in his beloved native country.

It was fortunate for him that just as he was about to start, Barker's patent Panorama of London was opened. Fulton adopted the device, and in Paris, taking out a patent of importation, engaged with a capitalist in building two Panoramas on the Boulevards, and from them opening the *passage Panorama*, a covered communication with a populous part of the city—the prototype of other *Arcades*. These statements I have from himself Thus furnished with the means, he prosecuted his studies, and afterwards, on his way to America, passing through London, was fortunate to buy, at Boydell's, the great pictures of "Lear in the Tempest," and the "Madness of Orphelia," by WEST, "Orlando," by Raphael West, and the original paintings, by SMIRKE, for Barlow's Columbiad. These pictures he liberally lent, during many years, to the Pennsylvania Academy of Fine Arts—an institution which I had originated, and for the commencement of which Mr. Joseph Hopkinson was induced to procure the necessary funds from his numerous friends. These are also historical facts, sufficiently interesting to be thus incidentally introduced It is due to the reputation of Mr. Fulton to say, that his most ardent ambition was *so* to employ his talents as to accumulate the means of promoting the Fine Arts, by the formation of a great Gallery of the choicest Works.

In the year 1807, on a visit which I paid to Mr. Fulton in New York, I found him seriously disturbed in his nerves, complaining of the *too kind* persecutions of his friends, who wished him to abandon his projects of Steam Navigation He told me they almost made him crazy. A few days after this, however, he invited me to a ship-yard on the East River, to witness his *first experimental demonstration* in America When I was admitted to the yard, to which only his intimate friends were invited, I perceived, some distance up the river, a common *flat bottomed scow*, with a number of persons on board, in the act of being turned round to return.   When it began to move, and advanced on the calm water, against the tide, at the rate of four miles an hour, it seemed like a huge tortoise, paddling onwards with its fore feet, and produced in me the most lively sensations As the scow touched the wharf, I jumped on a broad plank which crossed it midway, where Fulton stood alone, and seizing his hand, congratulated him on his success With stiffened arm energetically pressed downwards, he held my hand without reply, or regarding me, whilst his eye, during some moments, glanced from one *wheel*, across his steam pots, to the *other* wheel, each in diameter only four feet, and half submerged—then suddenly recognizing me, he gaily shook my hand, exclaiming—"Yes, now I have it, *they* (meaning the wheels, and throwing his hands aloft), *they* must be of *large* diameter, and but *little* sunk in the water." Those who would detract from Mr. Fulton's reputation, say, that in crossing the Atlantic, after the death of Mr Fitch, he became possessed of his papers and inventions—himself deserving no credit The *idea* of *water wheels*, instead of paddles, occurred to many, and doubtless to *Fitch*, at the time of his departure for England, but it will be manifest, that if Fulton took his *idea* from Fitch, *that idea* must have been to employ *small* wheels, which he used in his first experiments; and I am the *feeling* witness to declare, that whilst my hand was grasped in his, was the *moment* when the conviction flashed on his mind, that all that was necessary for the application of steam power to navigation, was to employ wheels of *large diameter*, and but little submerged.

Emboldened by his present success he immediately, in connection with Chancellor Livingston, engaged to build a steam-boat for the North River, which, on its first passage up, produced all the excitement which is so graphically described by Judge Story To Fulton it was the calm realization ot his hopes and purpose ; yet on the minds of those who had heard nothing of it previously, the appearance of such a wonderful novelty had all the charm of romance, which the historian was at liberty to describe, but not on his page to perpetuate the error that it was his first experiment It remains to the credit of America that she had the benefit of Steam Navigation *five* years before it was adopted in England.

I remain respectfully yours,

REMBRANDT PEALE.

V —*A letter from James Logan to the Society of Friends, on the subject of their opposition in the Legislature to all means for the Defence of the Colony, September 22, 1741.*

My Friends,—It is with no small Uneasiness that I find myself concerned to apply thus to this Meeting : but as I have been longer and more deeply engrossed in the Affairs of Government, and I believe I may safely say, have considered the Nature of it more closely than any Man besides in the Province ; as I have also from my Infancy been educated in the Way that I have since walked in, and I hope without Blemish, to the Profession ; I conceive and hope you will think I have a Right to lay before you the heavy Pressure of Mind that some late Transactions in this small Government of ours has given me ; through an apprehension, that not only the Reputation of Friends as a People, but our Liberties and Privileges in general may be deeply affected by them

But on this Head, I think fitt to mention in the first Place, that when above two and forty years since, our late Proprietor proposed to me at Bristol, to come over with him as his Secretary, after I had agreeably to his Advice taken time to consider of it, which I did very closely before I engaged, I had no scruple to accept of that, or of any other Post I have since held being sensible that as Government is absolutely necessary amongst Mankind, so, though all Government, as I had clearly seen long before, is founded on Force, there must be some proper Persons to administer it. I was therefore the more surprised, when I found my Master, on a particular occasion in our Voyage hither, though coming over to exercise the Powers of it in his own Person here, shewed his sentiments were otherwise : but as I have ever endeavoured to think and act consistently myself, observing that Friends had laid it down as a Principle that bearing of Arms even for Self-Defence is unlawful, being of a different Opinion in this respect, tho' I have ever condemned Offensive War, I therefore in a great Measure declined that due Attendance on their Meetings of Business that I might otherwise have given. I must here nevertheless add further, that I propose not in offering this, to advance Arguments in Support of the lawfulness of Self-Defence, which amongst those who for Conscience Sake continue in a Condition to put strictly in Practice the Precepts of our Saviour, would be altogether needless ; but wherever there is a Private Property, and Measures taken to increase it by amassing Wealth according to our Practice, to a Degree that may tempt others to invade it, it has always appeared to me to be full as Justifiable to use Means to defend it when gott, as to acquire it: Notwithstanding which I am sensible our Friends have so openly and repeatedly professed their Principles on that Head to the Government, and they have thereupon been so much distinguished by their Favours as a peaceable People, from whom no Plots or Machinations of any kind are to be feared, that I shall consider this, as I have said to be their standing and avowed Principle, and only offer to your Consideration, what I conceive to be a clear Demonstration, that all Civil Government as well as Military is founded on Force, and therefore the Friends as such in the strictness of their Principles, ought in no manner to engage in it; As also, that as We are a Subordinate Government, and therefore accountable to a Superior one for our Conduct. it is expected by that Superior, that this Province as well as all the other British Colonies shall make the best Defence against a Foreign Enemy in its Power, as it was required to do by the late Queen Anne in the last French War, upon which the then Governor raised a Militia of three Companies of Volunteers, but for Want of a Law for its support, it dropt in about two Years after—and the like Orders may undoubtedly be expected again, when another War with France breaks out which is said now to appear unavoidable. That it is of the greater Importance to Britain, as it is for other Reasons most assuredly to Ourselves that the Countrey should be defended, as it lies in the Heart of the other British Colonies on the Main And that it is well known in Europe that from the vast Conflux of People into it from Germany and Ireland, numbers who can bear Arms are not wanting for a Defence, were there a Law for it, as there is in all the other British Colonies, I think without an exception.

That all Government is founded on Force, and ours as well as others, will be indisputably evident from this—King Charles II., in his Grant of this Province to our Proprietor, directed that the Laws of England for the Descent of Land and the Preservation of the Peace, should continue the same, till altered by the Legislative Authority: and our Government continues on the same Plan, with Judges, Justices, Sheriffs, Clerks, Coroners, Juries, &c., all of whom who act by Commissioners, have them from the Governour in the English Form : the English Law is pleaded in all our Courts, and our Practitioners copy as near as they can after the Practice in Westminster Hall. By that Law, when the Peace is commanded even by a Constable, all Obedience to that Command manifestly arises from a Sense in the Person or Persons commanded that Resistance would be punished, and, therefore, they chuse to avoid it: but in Civil Cases of more importance the Sheriff who is the principal acting Officer executes the Judgments of the Court upon those they were given against, which they are obliged to comply with, how much soever against their will, for here also they know Resistance would be in vain; or if they attempt any, the Sheriff is obliged by the Law, without any Manner of Excuse, to find a sufficient Force, if to be had in his County, to compel to a Compliance. And in the Pleas as the Crown, besides that he is obliged to put to Death such Criminals of by the Law have been condemned to it, He, as general Conservator of the Peace, is likewise invested by the same Law with proper Powers for suppressing all Tumults, Riots, Insurrections and Rebellions on whatsoever Occasion they may arise, as far as the Posse or whole Force of his County may enable him, and for this end he receives, together with his Commission, the King's Writt of Assistance, requiring all Persons within his District, to be aiding to him in these and all other cases, by which if need be, they may freely use Fire Arms and all manner of destructive Weapons, and are not at all accountable by the Law for any Lives they may take of those in the Opposition, any more than a man is on the High Road for killing another who attempts to rob him. And such as refuse to assist the Sheriff are by the same Law liable to Fine and Imprisonment, from whence 'tis evident there is no Difference in the last Resort, between Civil and Military Government, and that the Distinction that some affect to make between the Lawfulness of the one and the other is altogether groundless—as none are killed in the Field, so none are punished with their Good will; a superior Force is employed in the one case as well as in the other, and the only difference that I have ever been able to discover in their Essentials is, that the Sheriff being but one Person in his County cannot possibly assemble any very great number together on any regular Method or Order, as in case of any Insurrection in the city Philadelphia would soon appear: but on the contrary in a regular Militia every man knows his commanding officer, and whither to repair on a proper call—and from these Premises it certainly follows that whoever can find Freedom in himself to join in Assembly in making Laws, as particularly for holding of courts, is so far concerned in Self-Defence, and makes himself essentially as obnoxious to censure as those who directly vote for it

But further, it is alledged that King Charles II. very well knew our Proprietor's Principles when he granted him the Powers of Government contained in the charter: To which 'tis answered, that amongst the other Powers granted to the Proprietor and his Deputies, He is created by the charter a Captain General with ample powers to levy War against any Nation or People not in Amity with the Crown of England, which in case he were not free to do by himself he might by his Deputies. and if he is invested with Powers to make an Invasive War, much more is it to be expected that he should defend his country against all Invaders. And I am a Witness that in those two years, or somewhat less, that the Proprietor took the Administration on himself when last here, He found himself so embarrassed between the indispensable Duties of Government on the one hand, and his Profession on the other, that he was determined if he had staid to act by Deputy.

It is further alledged by our Friends, that no other was expected than that this should be a Colony of Quakers, and it is so reputed to this day: that they are willing themselves to rely on the sole Protection of Divine Providence, and others who would not do the same should have kept out of it, for nobody called or invited them. But it is answered to this, That the King's Charter gives free leave to all his subjects without Distinction to repair to the country and settle in it · and more particularly the Proprietor's own Invitation was general and without exception: and by the Laws he had passed himself, no Country, no Profession whatever, provided they owned a God, were to be excluded. That 'tis true our Friends at first made a large Majority in the Province, but they are said now to make upon a moderate computation not above a Third of the Inhabitants: That although they alledge they cannot for conscience sake bear Arms, as being contrary to the peaceable Doctrine of Jesus Christ, (whose own Disciples nevertheless are known to have carried Weapons,) Yet without Regard to others of Christ's Precepts, full as express against laying up Treasure in this World, and not caring for To-morrow, they are as intent as any others, in amassing Riches, the great Bait and Temptation to our Enemies to come and plunder the Place · in which Friends would be very far from being the only sufferers, for their neighbours must equally partake with them, who therefore by all means desire a law for a Militia, in a regular Manner to defend themselves and the country as they have in the other Colonies

That in the last French War, Pensilvania was but an inconsiderable Colony, but now, by it's extended commerce, it has acquired a very great Reputation, and particularly that Philadelphia has the Name of a rich City, is known to have no manner of Fortification, and is, as has been said, a tempting Bait by Water from the Sea. and by Land the whole country lies exposed to the French, with whom a war is daily expected · That the French in their last War with England were so greatly distressed in Europe, by a current of yearly Losses, that they were glad to set quiet where they might, but now it is much otherwise, as they appear rather in a condition to give Laws to their Neighbours: That our Indians unhappily retiring Westward have opened a ready Road and Communication between this Province and Canada, by their settling at Allegheny, a branch of that great River Mississippi, which branch extending a thousand miles from it's Mouth where it enters the said River, reaches even into this Province, and between it's Waters, and the Western Branches of Susquehanna, there is but a small Land-carriage: That the French exceedingly want such a country as this to supply their Islands with provisions, and our Rivers for an easier Inlet into that vast country of Louisiana which they possess on Mississippi than they now have by the barred Mouth of it, that empties itself a great way within the shoal Bay of Mexico: and they have many large nations of Indians in Alliance with them, to facilitate their conquests: for all which Reasons our numerous back Inhabitants, as well as others, ought to be obliged to furnish themselves with arms, and to be disciplined as in other Colonies for their own proper Defence, which would be no Manner of charge to the Publick, and but little to Particulars.

These, I think, are the principal Arguments adduced by those who plead for a Law for Self-Defence, to which I shall add these other weighty considerations, that may more particularly affect Friends as a People.

The Government, and particularly the Parliament of Britain, appear to have this War very much at Heart, in which they spare no charge in fitting out large Fleets with Land Forces, and expect that all their Colonies will in the same Manner exert themselves, as the Assemblies of all the others have in some measure done, ours excepted, not only in their Contributions, but they have also generally a regular Militia for their Defence

Our Friends have recommended themselves to the Government not only by their peaceable Deportment, as has been already observed, but by complying with it's Demands in chearfully contributing by the payment of their Taxes towards every War Yet they are admitted into no Offices of the Government above those of the respective Parishes where they live, except that some have undertaken to receive Publick Money and though tolerated in their Opinions as they interfere not with the Administration; yet these Opinions are far from being approved by the Government, that when they shall be urged as a Negative to putting so valuable a country as this, and situate as has been mentioned, in a proper Posture of Defence, those who plead their Privileges for such a Negative, may undoubtedly expect to be divested of them, either by act of Parliament, or a Quo-Warranto from the King against their charter, for it will be accounted equal to betraying it And this, besides the irreparable Loss to ourselves, must prove a Reproach and vast Disadvantage to the Profession every where.

'Tis alledged the Governor made a false step last year, in encouraging or suffering our Servants to inlist, for which he has been abridged by the Assembly of the Salary for a year and a Half, that had for many years before been allowed to our Governors. But as this is interpreted by the Ministry as a Proof of his extraordinary Zeal for the King's Service, his conduct herein, as also his Letter to the Board of Trade, however displeasing to us, will undoubtedly recommend him the more to the Regard of our Superiors, in whose Power we are, and accordingly we may expect to hear of it

Our Province is now rent into Parties, and in a most Unchristian manner divided: Love and Charity, the grand characteristicks of the Christian Religion, are in a great measure banished from among the People, and contention too generally prevails: But for the weighty Reasons that have been mentioned in this Paper, it is not to be doubted that those who are for a Law for Defence, if the War continues and the country be not ruined before, must in Time obtain it. It is therefore proposed to the serious and most Weighty consideration of this Meeting, Whether it may not at this Time be advisable, that all such, who for conscience sake cannot joyn in any Law for Self-Defence, should not only decline standing Candidates at the ensuing Election of Representatives themselves, but

also advise all others who are equally scrupulous to do the same—and as Animosities and Faction have of late greatly prevailed amongst us, and at all times there prevails with too many, an ill-judged parsimonious Disposition, who for no other reason than to save their money, though probably on some other pretence, may vote for such as they may think by their opposition to the Governor, may most effectually answer that end : That such Friends should give out publickly before hand when they find they are named, that they will by no means stand or serve, though chosen : and accordingly—that the meeting recommend this to the Deputies from the several Monthly or Quarterly meetings in this Province—all which from the sincerest Zeal for the Publick Good, Peace of the Country, and not only the Reputation, but the most Solid Interest of Friends as a People, is (I say again) most seriously recommended to your consideration by
Your true Friend and Well wisher,

JAMES LOGAN.

STENTON Sept. 22, 1741.
To Robert Jordan and Others, the Friends of the Yearly Meeting for Business now convened at Philadelphia.

—

On examination of the Minutes of the Yearly Meeting for 1741, it appears that James Logan addressed a letter to Robert Jordan and others, which was produced to that Body. In conformity to custom in such cases, the paper was referred to a Committee and Samuel Preston and others were selected for the purpose of examining it, who reported " that the subject matter of the Letter related to the Civil and Military Affairs of the Government, and in their opinion it was unfit to be read to the Meeting."

Extract of a Letter of R. Peters to J. Penn.

The Yearly Meeting being held the Week before the general Election, Mr. Logan by his son William sent them a Letter, wherein he is said to enlarge on the defenceless state of the Province, and of the ill consequences that may ensue on men of their Principles procuring themselves to be returned to Assembly, but his good Design was eluded by the following expedient. Some Members moved that a Committee might be appointed to peruse the Letter, and to report whether it contained matters which were fit for the meeting to take into consideration—accordingly Rob't. Jordan, Jno. Bringhouse, Ebenezer Large, John Dillwin and Rob't. Strethill were appointed to inspect the Epistle, and report whether it contained matters proper to be communicated to the meeting at large. On examination they reported that the Letter containing matters of a Military and Geographical nature, it was by no means proper to be read to the general meeting, but some persons who understood those matters might be desired to consider and answer it. Rob't. Strethill singly declared that considering that Letter came from one who was known to have had abundance of experience, was an old member, and had a sincere affection for the Welfare of the Society, he was apprehensive should this Letter be refused a reading in the Meeting, such a proceeding would not only disgust him but the Body of Friends in England, especially as
4*

42

it might be supposed to contain several things that were intended for the good of the Society at these fickle and precarious times—but Jno. Bringhouse plucked him by the coat and told him with a sharp tone of voice, " Sit thee down Robert, Thou art single in thy opinion " Mr. Logan, in resentment as I suppose of such treatment caused thirty copies to be printed off to save the trouble of copying, with a design to send them to his friends in England, but whether he will or no is now doubtful, tho I will persuade him if possible to send one to the Proprietors. It is said, but I advance this without knowing anything from him of the matter that either by the persuasion of Mr. Logan or in a conference that was held at his house with some of the principal members of the Meeting, he has altered his mind, keeps the contents a secret, and is disposed to suppress the Whole. However he has promised the Governor, Mr Allen, and myself, the reading of it but under secrecy at this time which I can't account for.

NOTE

. The following passage from Franklin's Memoirs refers to what occurred between Penn and Logan on their voyage to America, and referred to above, (page 36 near the end)

" The Honorable and learned Mr. Logan, who had always been of that sect, wrote an address to them declaring his approbation of *defensive* war, and supported his opinion by many strong arguments: he put into my hands sixty pounds to be laid out in lottery tickets for the battery, with directions to apply what prizes might be drawn wholly to that service He told me the following anecdote of his old master, William Penn, respecting defence. He came over from England when a young man with that proprietary, and as his secretary. It was war time, and their ship was chased by an armed vessel, supposed to be an enemy. The captain prepared for defence, he told William Penn and his company of Quakers that he did not expect their assistance, and that they might retire into the cabin, which they did, except James Logan, who chose to stay on deck and was quartered to a gun. The supposed enemy proved a friend, so there was no fighting: but when the Secretary went down to communicate the intelligence, William Penn rebuked him severely for staying upon deck and undertaking to assist in defending the vessel contrary to the principle of Friends, especially as it had not been required by the captain. This reprimand being before all the company, piqued the secretary, who answered: " I being thy servant, why did thee not order me to come down, but thee was willing enough that I should stay and help fight the ship when thee thought there was danger."

VI —*Accounts of the Overseers of the Poor of the City of Philadelphia,* (*March 29th,* 1758, *to March 25th,* 1759.)

[These accounts are kept in Pennsylvania currency, in which one pound was equal to two dollars and sixty-six and two-thirds cents of our present currency.

City of Philadelphia for Disbursements for the Poor.

1758	DR.	£	s.	d
March 29	To Cash to Hannah Catt		5	
30	Camphor			6
31	Cash to Catharine Denny for nursing an orphan child 2 weeks		10	
April 3	2½ cords of wood, cording, &c	1	14	2
4	A tin lanthorn,		4	
	Pieces green binding, 4s., 1 piece colored thread, 4s.		8	
5	12¼ lbs. flax, a 1s.		12	3
	Sending a woman out of town, charge		1	9
	" Hannah Kenny and child out of town		5	
6	15 bushels turnips a 1s. 2d.		17	6
7	4 loads tan and wheeling		4	
	Haling Ellis Havord's goods to Alms House		2	
	C. Priscilla Cowley for nursing and laying out Elizabeth Havord		11	6
	Jas. Rumidge's charge going into the country		1	
	Catharine Denny 1 week nursing a child		5	
11	Haling McLoud's goods to yᵉ Alms House		1	6
12	Cash to Hannah Catt		5	
	2 qts oatmeal 1s. 4d., ½ pt neatsfoot oil 1s 4d.		2	8
13	Hugh Crott's charges to Burlington		2	
	John Jervis's bill for books, &c.	4	9	
14	Catharine Denny 1 week nursing a child		5	
	2 pieces check linnen bought at vendue	2	18	8
15	Carter's bill for haling, &c.	1	1	
19	Expenses removing a woman with a blind child to Burlington		6	
	1 lb. butter, 1s., camphor, 6d		1	6
	Vial sp sal vol., 9d., 1 lb rosin, 4d.		1	1
21	2 cords wood, and cording, 4d. a 12s	1	4	4
24	3½ yds linnen for a shirt for Hugh Crott, a 3s.		10	6
25	Hannah Catt 2 weeks nursing a child, a 5s.		10	
	Jacob Turner		5	
	Peter Fretter, mending spinning wheels		5	
	Mary Pane yᵉ Midwife for delivering a woman		10	
27	Charles Dickinson, assisting him to go to Maryland		7	6
	12 cedar posts and haling		13	6
May 1	Jane Hart for keeping Robt. Muron a little boy		2	6

City of Philadelphia for the Poor.

1758		DR.	£	s.	d.
May	2	To David Cummins for keeping Sus. Brownhold 1 year	3		
	3	To Margaret Low		1	6
		1½ cord wood and cording		19	9
		A cow	6		
		Pieces of linen for Barnett's shift necks			9
	4	Hannah Catt, one week nursing a child		5	
	7	2 negroes wheeling Catharine Shannon to Alms House		1	6
	8	Turning an old beggar out of town 1s., his coffee 1s. 2d.		2	2
	10	6 cords wood and cording, a 11s. 2d.	3	7	
	11	4½ " "	2	10	3
		William Shipley's account to this date	31	17	3
		Hannah Catt one week nursing a child		5	
		2 c. 1 qr. rice of Jos. Reynolds, a 13s.	1	10	1
		2 poor women		2	6
	13	13 yds ticking a 1s.		13	
		Lydia Ellis		2	
		9 cords wood and cording a 10s. 2d.	4	11	6
	15	Samuel Crispin for Margaret Grant's child's coffin		5	
		8 c 1 qr old junk of Lightfoot's, a 7s. 6d	3	1	10
		Haling do. to Alms House		1	6
	16	77 ells ozinbrigs of Ogden & Hewes, a 19d	6	1	11
	17	¼ cord of wood to Mary Mackinary, a woman lying in		7	10
		Jas. Davis's account for making a fence	2	5	8
		5 cords wood and cording, a 11s. 2d.	2	15	10
	18	Peter Fretter, mending spinning wheel		2	
		Hannah Catt, one week nursing child		5	
		1 gallon train oil of David Deshler		3	
		Granny Ganderwitt for laying Mary Mackinary		10	
	19	1 lb pepper 3s. 6d, red precipitate 6d.		4	
		Mary Mackinary, lying in		5	
		5¼ cords wood and cording, a 10s. 2d.	2	13	5
	20	4 yds. coarse linen, a 9d.		3	
	21	Barbara Charleton, assisting her towards Lancaster		1	
	22	Eliza Bell for Jane Kelly's rent		15	
		William Brown's account for flour	21	12	
	23	Mary Mackinary's being nursed, for which I paid the nurse		7	
		Mary Gaffy		1	
		Ann Richardson		2	6
		8 cords wood and cording, a 11s. 2d.	4	9	4

45

City of Philadelphia for the Poor.

1758	DR	£	s.	d.
May 24	To Charles Smith for mending wheelbarrows		5	
	Margaret Camphle, to send her out of town		2	
	John Morton for Math. Stacey's quarter rent		10	
	Haling Michael Wharton's goods to James Eddy		1	6
25	6 c. 2 qrs middlings, and porterage 1s. 6d., at 11s	3	18	
	6 bbls. rye meal, *a* 1s.	2	2	
	Hannah Catt for this and the ensuing week's nursing child, 10s., calico for child, 2s. 8d.		12	8
26	14¾ cords wood and cording, *a* 11s. 2d.	8	4	8½
	Ruth Freeman for Nicholas Wharton's rent	1	5	
	7¾ yds. linsey woolen, *a* 2s 8d	1		8
27	Mary Mackinary		5	
	Mary Pain for laying Ann Morrison		10	
	Mary McGaffy		2	
	Wm. Peters for taking McLoud to workhouse		1	6
	Jos. Yarnell's account for carting	5	1	6
29	Vinegar		1	2
	Margaret Yard's charges to Newtown		1	6
	Physick for a poor woman			9
31	39 c 25 qrs. middlings, *a* 11s.	21	11	4
	A poor family in Hall's Alley		1	
June 3	Benj. Fuller's account for 265½ yds dowlass	16	6	3
5	Dougherty Jones's account for shoes	3	18	
	Mary McGaffy		2	
7	Ann Fitzgarell, assisting her to New York		5	
	16½ cords wood and cording	9	1	6
8	Hannah Catt for nursing child this week and ye next		10	
	100 rails	1	5	
9	6 yds. linen for shift necks, *a* 3s. 6d.	1	1	
	Wm. Purcill 2s., ʒi cerat trinr 6d		2	6
	4½ cords wood and cording	2	10	3
10	John Rowen's charge 3s 4d for taking Ann Auborn on the road to Chester, to her child		3	6
	Charge in binding out Mary Fitzsimmons	1		
13	Mary Gaffy		2	
	8 cords wood and cording	4	9	4
14	John Yarnell's account for haling	3	10	
	Sundry check linen bought at vendue	4	3	2½
16	Wm. Pristle		2	
17	Elizabeth Ben's rent paid to Wm. Keith		15	
19	Mary Gaffy		2	
22	Hannah Catt for nursing child this and ye ensuing week		10	

City of Philadelphia for the Poor.

1758	DR.	£	s	d.
June 22	To expenses in transporting Jno. Hayns' wife and child to Motherkill		11	6
23	Rum at haymaking		3	
	Pair shoes to Thomas Ashton		8	
	Henry Mansfield		2	
24	Vinegar		1	
	Jas. Campbell's expenses in getting him into ye Hospital, being a released captive		2	6
25	A pair trowsers for James Downey		6	
	Mark Miller, mowing lot at Alms House		9	
27	Mary Gaffy		2	
	3½ cords of wood and cording, a 11s. 2d.	1	19	1
28	Wm Brown for flour, as per Jas. Eddy's order,	9		
	7 cords wood and cording, a 11s. 2d	3	18	2
	Linen frock for Samuel Hopkins		6	
	William Carr, for getting his saw mended		3	6
	Jane Welsh for Adams, (blind,) quarter's rent	1	15	
	Henry Mansfield		2	
July 1	Deborah Yieldhall, expenses to Brunswick		4	
	James Baxter, for his quarter's salary, &c.	7	12	8
3	Lime and white-wash brush		7	
6	Hannah Catts nursing a child this and ye next week		10	
	Sending a man into the Jerseys			9
7	Wm. Keith for Eliza Benn's iron pot		5	
	John Wallace's bill for wood, being 12 cords	6	10	3
8	Henry Wolley (a poor man)		2	6
	1 liquorice ball to W. Dod 4d., shiftnecks to M Neal 6d.			10
10	Wm Plumstead for administering to Eliza Havords		17	
	Sending Robert Morris, from the workhouse, over Schuylkill		2	
11	John Hill's account for coffins	4	16	
14	John Kelfe's account for 160 ells oznbrigs a 18d.	12	13	4
	Amount of pension book from March ye 31st to June ye 23d	67	14	
	A dose rhubarb for a poor woman		1	3
20	1 yard linen for womens' shift necks		3	6
	Hannah Catts nursing a child this and ye next week		10	
25	1 hhd molasses of 91 gallons of Wm. Jackson, a 2s 7d.	11	15	1
26	Edward Harrington, for Mary McInary's rent	1		

City of Philadelphia for the Poor.

1758	DR.	£	s	d.
July 26	Butter for Catharine Holliday, lying in		1	
	John Hill's charge in going to Northampton		9	
	Moses Foster, for conveying a D. woman out of town		2	
27	Eliza Lindsey, to recover her clothes, and subsistence some time in the country		10	
	Aq. Cerrap's nigr. for ye alms house		1	6
29	Mary Pain, for delivering Eliza Gibbons		10	
31	Eleanor Hopkins, cash		5	
	Ann Copeland, "		1	9
Aug. 1	Jno. Rowen, for removing Ann Copeland and Mary Copeland out of town		10	
	Jno. Baxter, for boards for hog pen		3	5
2	Cash for butter to Eliza Gibbons		1	
	Jno Hill		16	6
3	Hannah Catt, for nursing child this and ye next week		10	
8	2 doses salts			8
9	Marg Ewe's charges to Burlington		5	
	James Rumidge		1	
10	John Yarnell's account for carting	5	9	6
	Carrying a woman to work-house			6
11	Sending Mary Mullon and 2 children out of town		1	1
	Duncan Leech's account for haling 31 loads tan	2	16	6
	1 oz. liquorice balls to W. Koiler			4
	Vial drops to Susanna Perkins		1	
14	George Gibson, to pay for lodging 6d., 1 lb. sal. eps. 4d.			10
16	A linen frock for Isaac Corren		5	
17	H. Catt, for nursing child this week and ye next		10	
	Granny Pauling for laying Cath Holliday		10	
18	A pair shoes for Matthew Stacey		8	
21	189 gallons molasses, bought of Robert Jepson, a 2s. 6d	23	12	6
	Haling ditto to alms house		3	
	Eliza Blair, cash		5	9
	do. a bottle Godfrey's cordial		1	3
23	Doughty Jones's account for shoes	2	6	
26	Sarah Howell, for making Cath. Atkinson's gown		2	6
	Jno Morton, for Matthew Stacey's quarter's rent		10	
29	Eliza Blair, cash		5	

1758	DR.	£	s.	d.
Aug. 29	To Charges in sending Phebe Hervey out of town		3	9
30	A bottle sweet oil for yᵉ alms house		2	6
31	Cath. Dardis, for Mary McGaffy's quarter's rent		5	
	Hannah Catt, for this and yᵉ next week, nursing child		10	
Sept. 5	Mary Hobbins, cash		1	
	Charges of warrant and serving, against Ch. Neal		1	9
7	Peter Hines, for Mary Hobbins's accommodation		5	
10	Elizabeth Blair, cash		2	6
	Physick for yᵉ flux, to Mary Gaffy's child		1	
14	Hannah Catt, nursing child this and yᵉ next week		10	
15	Jas. Eddy's order		7	
	Peter Hines, for Mary Hobbins's accommodation		5	
	Lydia Eller's sick child, cash		2	6
16	Hannah Catt, for a sick child		5	
22	17 cwt., 3 qrs., 4 lbs., Midlings, of James McTare, *a* 8s. 9d.	7	15	7½
	Peter Hines, for Mary Hobbins's accommodation		5	
	Jas. Davis's account for Carpenter's wharf	10	11	11
23	Eliza Carter, cash, per order		2	
26	John Crepson's account	2		
	Jas. Whitehead's account	1	2	8
	Hannah Catt, for yᵉ sick child		1	6
28	Lydia Ellis, for her sick child		2	6
	Jas. Eddy's order		1	10
29	Granny Paul, for laying L. Loyd		10	
30	Wm. Shipley's account for meat	61	5	9
	Mary Hobbins, for her accommodations		5	
	Hannah Catt, for nursing child this and yᵉ next week		15	
Oct. 2	John Baxtors, for his quarter's salary, &c.	8	7	
	Jane Welsh, for Wm. Adams' quarter's rent	1	15	
3	Thos. Gregory's account for casting bell for the alms house, deducting for old bell	5	1	3
	Amount of pension book from June yᵉ 30th to Sept. 22d	63	13	6
7	Cash to poor woman and child		2	6
9	do. to Henry Smith, his wife and child sick		2	6
10	Pocket book, for poor use, 3s. 9d., and for lb. caudles for tailor at almshouse		4	6

City of Philadelphia for the Poor

1758	DR.	£	s.	d
Oct. 12	To Charges attending ye discovery and appre-hending Pleasant Stratton	2		
13	John Hill's account for coffins, &c.	3	5	
	Eliza Carpenter, in Hall's alley		2	6
14	26 1 0 of hay, weighing and hauling to alms house	3	4	0½
19	Vial gutt pectoral for Wm. Herbert		1	6
	Cash to Jane Clark, moving her, with two chil-dren, out of town		2	6
	do. to Mary Yard, do.			10
	Cash to Eliza Carpenter, in H. alley		2	6
	do to Mary Pane, for laying of Catharine Cosgrove		10	
21	Cash to Margaret Allen, a sick woman, to con-vey her to Burlington; ʒi liquorice		2	10
	Cash to Elinor Hopkins		1	1
23	do. to Daniel Goodman, for Ea. Carpenter		10	0
	do for qt. of rum for tailor		1	1
24	do to Wm. Fest, for sweeping chimney at alms house		7	6
25	do. paid Paul Beck's account for 11 days tailor's work at alms house, a 2s. 4d	1	5	8
26	do to John Rowan, for conveying Thos Trip out of town		2	
31	do. for load of tan for Perkins, and vial sp. camphor, a 9d		2	3
	do. to Hannah Pearson, for part curing Mary Carter's scald head	1	10	
	do. for 9 cwt 1 qr middlings, a 10s. 6d.	4	17	1
Nov 1	do. for 17 cwt. 2 qrs. do. a 10s.	8	15	
	do to John Rowan moving Cath. Cosgrove		2	
7	do. for 1 doz. pewter spoons		4	
9	do. for 31¾ yds. of Linsey of James Miller, a 2s. 6d.	3	19	4½
10	do. for 2 ps. worsted quality's binding		8	
11	do. for 7 yards of linsey woolsey, a 2s. 5d.		16	11
12	do. for 8¼ yards do. a 2s. 4d.		19	3
17	do. for ʒss. camphor to Belandi Millar		1	
18	do. to Capt. Campbell, freight for Rachel Me-guire and children to Carolina	1	7	
25	do. to Wm. Young, earthenware for a horse	1	3	10
28	do. gave a poor woman		1	
	do. Paul Beck, for making 2 coats and 2 pair of breeches	1	2	
29	do. for warrant and serving on John Kearns		1	8
Dec 1	do to Hannah Sawer, just laid in		3	3

City of Philadelphia for the Poor.

1758	DR.	£	s.	d.
Dec. 4	To cash for digging grave for Wm. Herbert at the Presbyterian burial ground		4	6
6	do. 11 yards of linsey woolsey, *a* 2s. 6d.	1	7	6
7	do. for 7 cwt. 2 qrs. middlings, *a* 11s.	4	2	6
8	do. to Bridget Asbee, come from hospital		2	6
10	do. to Mary Brown, ill of yᵉ flux		2	6
11	do. to Jon. Guest, for pair shoes for Mary Koyle's child		3	6
	do. to Mary Betterton for bread, on account of Wm. Carter's donation to yᵉ poor	3		
	do. paid John for giving publick notice		1	6
12	do. paid John Hill, for coffins, &c.	3		
14	do. Doughty Jones, his bill for shoes	9	16	6
16	do. to Diana McCulough, quarter's rent for Eliza. Carter		17	6
	do. for 18 yards linsey woolsey, *a* 2s. 6d.	2	5	
	do. to poor woman, to pay for lodging			4
18	do. paid Joseph Harmer for half year's rent of Michael Walton	1	6	
20	20 cwt. 2 qrs. 21 lbs. middlings, *a* 10s. 9d.	11	2	5
23	Cash to convey Mary Neal out of town		3	
26	do. to Ed. Beach's wife		12	
	do. to James Hunter, for 2 doz. of men's stockings, *a* 35s. 6d.	3	11	
	George Morrison's account	32	12	1½
27	Cash for ferriage 2 women to yᵉ Jerseys			8
28	do. for 3½ napt cloth for boy at hospital		16	10
	do. for 1½ oznabrigs for do.		2	
	Amount of pension book to yᵉ 15th instant	57	13	11
29	Cash to Granny Pauling, for laying Peg Neal		10	
	do. for 2¼ yards oznabrigs for alms house		3	
	do. to John Baxter, his quarter's salary to the 29th inst., and his other account	8	10	6
30	do. to Joseph Mattson's wife and children		2	6
	do. to Rosemariui Burd		2	2
1759				
Jan. 2	do. to Jane Welsh, quarter's rent for Adams, yᵉ blind man	1	15	
	do. for taking man to workhouse, and conveying him from there to Charleston		3	6
	do. for ps. worsted binding for almshouse		4	
	do. paid John Hill, his bill	4	2	6
4	do. to Wm. Shipley, his bill to yᵉ 27th Dec.	50		
	5 yards broad cloth for two men's coats	1	15	
	5 yards oznabrigs for the above, and lining 2 pairs of breeches		6	

City of Philadelphia for the Poor.

1759	DR.	£	s.	d.
Jan. 5	To cash for petticoat for Farrell's child		1	9
	do. gave a poor woman			6
6	do paid Richard Howard, for making sundry clothes for poor	1	6	10
13	do. paid John Morton, quarter's rent for Matt. Stacey		10	
	do. gave James Kelly		2	6
	do. gave Rosemarini Burd		2	
14	do. to Rachel Loftus, for making Eliza Lindsey's gown		3	
	do. to Joseph Mattson's wife		2	
	dy. to Dorothy Lunan, ye smith's wife		2	6
18	do. for oatmeal for alms house			8
21	do. paid for sweeping chimney at alms house		7	6
	do gave Jeptha Smith		2	
27	do gave John Burden, his family very sick		5	
29	do. to John Hill's account	2	12	6
31	do for 12 yards linsey woolsey, a 2s. 6d.	1	10	
Feb. 1	do. gave Eliza Knowland's child		2	6
	do. for 12 cwt. 2 qrs. 20 lbs. Middlings, a 11s.	7	3	9
	do. paid George Fudge for oven		10	
	do. paid for burial of Ann Barrett from Hospital		17	
	do. paid Rachel Gardner, for laying Mary Dawson, 10s and gave her 5s		15	
6	do. paid Mary Betterton for bread, being part of Wm Carter's donation	3		
	do. paid John for publishing do.		1	6
	do to Mary Dawson, lying in		5	
	20¼ yards of oznabrigs for 3 shirts, 2 shifts, and 1 apron, a 1s. 4d.	1	7	
7	do paid Duncan Leech for 4 loads of dung, to make hot-bed at alms house	1		
8	do. for 6 cwt. middlings of Josiah Jackson, a 11s. 6d.	3	9	
12	do. to Mary Dawson		5	
	do. to Isaac Moss, for Thos. Dodge's Coffin		12	6
15	do. to Mary Catin, with blind child		5	
	do. for 4 yards oznabrigs for a shift for Rachel Glover		5	4
17	do paid Isaac Greenleaf, on the hospital account for our patients	13	4	6
20	do. to Mary Dawson		5	
	do. to Joseph Howel's account for leather	1	13	11
22	Expenses for burial of Ed. Pitts		12	6

City of Philadelphia for the Poor.

1759	DR.	£	s.	d.
Feb 23	Cash to Mary Agnew		1	
	do. to Eliza Beiry's sick child		3	6
26	do. to Samuel Wotherd, mending pump		5	
	do. to Mary Dawson		5	
27	Ferriage of Alice Holland to yᵉ Jerseys			4
	Liquorice ball for several in the alms house		2	
	Robert Finch		2	6
March 3	Cash gave a poor man and his wife		1	6
	Hauling meal to yᵉ alms house		1	4
9	Amount of pension book from Dec. 22d, 1758, to March yᵉ 9th, 1759	57	14	6
10	3 yards linsey, for alms house, a 2s. 6d.		7	6
	Mary Dodge, her children sick		1	6
	Marg't Neal, cash		1	
14	Doughty Jones's account for shoes		19	5
15	Cash paid William Moses for William Hoskin's clothes		13	
16	Margaret Neal, cash		1	
17	Jerem. Halden's wife, cash		2	
	Cash to Mary Bourns for keeping a child, called Hannah Baker, 32 weeks, a 3s.	4	16	
	Eliza Lindsey, cash		2	6
	Marg't Neal, do		1	
20	Jas. Whitehead's account	4	1	10
21	Ephr. Smith's account for meal	8	15	
23	Matthew Stacey's rent, paid to Jno. Morton		10	
	2 ps. cotton romalls, bot of R. & Ab. Usher	2	4	
	Errata June 8th		10	
	Benj Marshall's account for sundries, Aug 16		1	
	Tin ware for alms house		8	
	John Hill's account for coffins	2	17	6
	John Baxton's account, with quarter's salary	8	3	10
	Dung for yᵉ garden	1	16	
	Granny Pauling for laying Sall Lunan		10	
	Coffin and digging grave for M. Stacey's wife		17	
	do. do. Jeptha Smith		17	
26	William Shipley's account for meat	54	15	9
	Benj Loxly's account of boards for yᵉ fence	1	11	
	Jas. Trueman, for 4¼ bush turnips		4	6
	2 week's pension, taken from yᵉ book, from yᵉ 16th to yᵉ 20th inst	9	7	
	Duncan Leech, for hauling dung to alms house	1	15	
	Valent Smith, for ditto	1	17	6
	John Hood for ditto, and wood to pensioners	6	12	
	Hugh Forbes for tubs, &c, for yᵉ house	2	5	
	Jacob Shoemaker's account for burials	6	9	6

City of Philadelphia for the Poor.

1759	DR.	£	s.	d.
March 26	Thos. Clifford's account, paid per yᵉ Mayor's order	10	18	9
	Hospital account against Mary Boardman, 7 weeks	1	8	
	George Morrison's account	14	10	1
	Dr. Shippen's salary	50		
		1103	4	10
	To our commissions on £1189, *a* 9*d* per £	44	11	9
	Balance due	41	4	2
		1189	00	9

Errors excepted.

April yᵉ 20th, 1759.

CHRISTOPHER MARSHALL,
'JAMES EDDY,
HUGH FORBES.

——

Philada ss.   Aug. 20th, 1759

Please to pay Robert Towers, William Faulkner, James Stevenson and James James, Overseers of the City Poor, the sum of Fifty pounds 6s. 1½d., being the balance settled and remaining in your hands.

THO. LAWRENCE, Mayor.

To Christopher Marshall,
    James Eddy,
    George Morrison,   } Late Overseers of the City Poor.
    Hugh Forbes

[Endorsed thereon.]

Received from Mr. Christopher Marshall, Fifty pounds, six shillings and one penny half penny, the contents of the within order

£50, 6s., 1d.

JAS. STEVENSON

Sept. 1st, 1759.

City of Philadelphia for the Poor.

1758		CR	£	s	d.
April 10	By Cash of Robt Strettle, fining a woman for swearing			5	
11	" Jno McMichael for non-attendance on jury		1		
	" Thos Lawrence for non-attendance on jury		1		
12	" Jacob Duchee for fining Ralph Collins for swearing			10	
28	" James Eddy		2		
May 10	" George Morrison		231	14	6
17	" James Eddy		220		6
June 22	" Jacob Duchee for a fine collected by him		1		
30	" George Morrison		1	14	6
July 5	" Joseph Merriott		32	6	11
11	" Jno Hill for ground rent of Wm. Carter's legacy due to the old overseers		2	4	
	" Jno. Hill for ground rent of Wm. Carter's legacy due to us		2	12	
15	" Sarah Steward for quarter's rent of house late Eliza Havord's		1	15	
22	" Capt Mitchell for expenses in burying of John Lindsey		1		1
	" Capt. Mitchell, his fine for swearing three oaths			15	
	" Jane Kelly for ye rent we paid for her			15	
24	" John Dalvil, his fine for swearing			15	
25	" George Morrison		114	14	6
28	" Thos Fisher for delivering two sows taken up for the poor ye belonging to Wm Ranberry			15	
29	" James Welsh for entertaining M Collins		1		
Aug. 2	" Widow woman for restoring a little black pig taken to ye Alms House			7	6
5	" George Adam Hough for restoring him two pigs taken up to ye Alms House			10	
7	" John Baxter for 200 lbs. oakum at 3½d		2	18	4
8	" Dr Edward Shippen, Jr., 5 fines, viz.: Aquila Jones, George Bryan, Thos. Smith, John Jones and John Jennings, for refusing to serve as constables, at £5 each		25		

City of Philadelphia for the Poor.

1758		CR.	£	s.	d.
Aug. 11	By Cash of	Wm. ———, butcher, for restoring five little pigs		8	10
15	"	Thos. Parson for restoring sow and pig		10	
23	"	George Boardman for 22 weeks for his mother Mary Boardman being in yᵉ hospital from April yᵉ 1st. to Sept. 2 *a* 2s. per week.	2	4	
24	"	John Stamper for fines collected of some person for profane swearing	1	5	
	"	Thomas Manney for ½ years' ground rent, being part of William Carter's legacy	2	12	
28	"	Yᵉ Mayor for a fine rec'd of Mary Zebulun for entertaining negroes	1		
Sept. 1	"	James Eddy	123	16	
15	"	John Stamper being a fine		10	
18	"	Daniel Dupree for an old pair shoe			
	"	buckles and gold ring lately belonging to William Allison dec'd	1	5	9
23	"	William Cockbour for swearing	1		
	"	John Stamper he rec'd for do.		5	
	"	Peter Barry		4	
28	"	John Cormick by the hands of David Thompson for Mary Redman's expenses while in alms house	4	15	
30	"	William Shipley for cow	4		
	"	Peter Barry		8	
Oct. 7	"	Mary Chesnell for entertaining a strange woman		13	
9	"	Peter Barry		4	
12	"	Yᵉ Mayor, Thomas Lawrence, a fine he rec'd for profane swearing		5	
16	"	David Welsh for five weeks of his child in the alms house *a* 3s. 6d.		17	6
20	"	The Mayor a fine for petty larceny		5	
26	"	Rudolph fine for Pr. swearing		5	
31	"	Mary Pemlet for being in alms house some time		16	
Nov. 1	"	Yᵉ Mayor a fine he received of Capt. Gash for refusing to entertain yᵉ officers billitted on him	3		
3	"	James Claxton for P. swearing		5	
	"	Yᵉ Mayor a fine of James Parrock for refusing to serve constable	5		
6	"	Yᵉ Mayor for restoring 2 pigs to yᵉ owner		10	

City of Philadelphia for the Poor.

1758		CR.		s.	d.
Nov. 6	By cash of	Jane White on acount of Catherine Cosgrove	1	7	
9	"	James Coultass late Sheriff, being a fine paid by Laughlane McClane for kissing of Osborne's wife, after his commissions and writing bond was deducted	24	5	
10	"	Sarah Steward a quarter's rent due 11th of Sept. for house late Eliza Havord	1	15	
18	"	Annia Boles for firing chimney	1		
	"	Henry Bowman for firing chimney	1		
25	"	Mayor for fines for P. swearing		10	
	"	George Morrison fine for short cord wood rec'd of Joseph Allen	2	10	
28	"	Jacob Duche a fine for a person entertaining McKnight's negro woman		10	
Dec. 1	"	Yᵉ Mayor for fines he received	1	15	
	"	James Eddy on account of Jon. Kearns	1		
	"	James Eddy on poor account		1	10
4	"	Yᵉ Mayor for fines he rec'd		10	
6	"	John Stamper for fines he rec'd		15	
10	"	Yᵉ Mayor for fines for P. swearing		15	
12	"	Ed. Beach for one mo. providing for his wife due this day, to be continued		12	
	"	John Mitchel on John Kearns' acc't		10	
26	"	George Morrison, including his acc't	65		
30	"	Joseph Morris, ground rent W. C.	6		
1759					
Jan. 6	"	For pigs delivered		4	6
	"	For poor sailor of Capt. Farris		10	
	"	Hospital collections	1	7	6
8	"	For box sold belonging to William Herbet		5	
21	"	Susa Steward, rent for Havord Hay	1	10	
	"	Joseph Willingpott for P. swearing		10	
29	"	John Heathcote one year's ground rent	1	10	
	"	For profane swearing		5	
Feb. 1	"	Jacob Shoemaker for 3 years' ground rent to the 5th of January, 1758 a 30s.	4	10	

City of Philadelphia for the Poor.

1759		CR.	£	s.	d.
Feb. 1	By cash of	David Welsh for his child being in the alms house	2	12	6
	"	George Boardman for 22 weeks for his mother Mary Boardman, in yᵉ hospital from Sept. 1, to this date *a 2s.*	2	4	
8	"	Fine of Robert Strettle for petty larceny		5	
	"	For old chest at alms house		15	
10	"	James Eddy	72	16	3
22	"	Alice Jeffy's father		10	3
28	"	Jeremiah Halden for his wife's accommodation in yᵉ alms house	2	10	
March 6	"	Yᵉ Mayor for fines rec'd for profane swearing	1	10	
8	"	Israel Dawes for maintaining and other charges on child Hannah Little	11		
10	"	Half a year's ground rent for a lot in Second street, being Carter's donation rec'd of Richard Robinson	5	4	
	"	Nicholas Stonemate for our right in yᵉ lease of a house late belonging to Eliza Havord, deceased	7		
14	"	Cameron & Drinker for ground rent in Race street, being Carter's donation	3	6	8
	"	Jeremiah Halden for his wife's accommodations in yᵉ alms house	1	10	
16	"	Sarah Steward for rent of a house late Eliza Havord's, deceased	1	18	
20	"	Jno. Stampers for fines received		15	
21	"	William Jackson, Edward Kearney, Andrew Reed, David Hall, John Fisher, Mordecai Yarnall and Reuben Heyns, being a fine for each of their chimneys being fired each *a 20s*	7		
22	"	—— Morton for four weeks accommodations for his wife in yᵉ alms house		12	
	"	George Boardman for his mother's accommodation in the hospital 7 weeks *a 2s.*		14	
23	"	David Welsh for 7 weeks accommodation for his child in yᵉ alms house *a 3s*	1	1	

City of Philadelphia for the Poor

1759		CR.	£	s.	d.
March 23	"	For 8 cwt. oakum *a* 26s.	3	18	
	"	150 lbs. oakum	1	16	
26	"	Joseph Thomas, flour brander	13	15	10
	"	Joseph King, late do.	27	5	3
	"	Jno. Cresson for Solomon's accommodation in yᵉ alms house	2		6
	"	Tax collected by George Morrison	36	17	1
	"	Jacob Shoemaker for one year's ground rent of a lot at Center, Carter's donation	1	10	
	"	Philip Kensey for his negro in alms-house	1	12	
	"	James Eddy	47	15	
	"	David Sheller's note of hand rec'd	2	1	3
	"	Jeremiah Halden, part of his note	1	2	6
	"	Nicholas Stonemate's note rec'd		12	
	"	Ground rent Carter's legacy due by William Logan	2	15	
			1189	00	10
Aug. 6	"	Balance brought forward	41	4	2½
	"	This sum short cash in one of the duplicates	9	1	11
	"	Balance to paid the succeeding overseers	50	6	1½
Sept. 1	"	Paid James Stevenson the above balence being £50 6s.1½d.			

VII.—*Proclamations by the Provincial Governors and Councils of Pennsylvania.*

(From the originals in the possession of the Society.)

1 A Proclamation continuing persons who were in office at the decease of Lieut. Governor Andrew Hamilton, in their respective posts:

THE GREAT
SEAL OF
PENNSYLVANIA.

By the President and Council for ye Government of ye Province of Pensilvania and Counties annexed

A PROCLAMATION.

FORASMUCH as it hath pleased Almighty God in his all-seeing Providence to Remove from us by Death our late Lieut. Governor, Col. Andrew Hamilton, And Whereas by Virtue of a Commission from William Penn, Esq , True and Absolute Proprietary and Governor in Chief of this Province of Pensilvania and Territories thereunto belonging, under his Hand and Great Seal, bearing date ye twenty-eighth day of October, One Thousand Seven Hundred and One, all and singular ye Powers, Jurisdictions, and Authorities whatsoever, necessary for ye well Governing of ye said Province and Territories, and for ye Administering, Maintaining, and Executing of Justice, and providing for ye safety and well being of ye People, are upon our said Lieut. Governor's decease devolved upon us, ye Council, Nominated and Appointed for ye same. We, therefore, ye said Council, in our care for ye welfare of ye State and Government of ye said Province and Territories, and to prevent all failures in ye Administration of justice therein, that might be occasioned by ye aforesaid Governor's decease, Doe hereby Ordain and Declare that all Commissions Whatsoever issued by ye said Lieut Governor during his administration of ye said Government, shall be, continue and remain, in full force and Virtue till further order shall be given in and about ye Same, and that all Persons Whatsoever who have or enjoy any Place, Post or Benefit, by Virtue of any Commission under our said Late Lieut Governor, Shall Continue to Enjoy ye same until they be Determined as aforesaid. And we doe further Charge and Require all Magistrates, Officers, and Commissioners whatsoever, who act by any Commission Derived from our said Proprietary and Governor. that they diligently Proceed in ye Performance of their Respective Trusts and Charges in ye said Government, for ye safety and well being thereof Given under our Hands and ye great Seal of ye Government at the

Council Chamber in Philadelphia, yᵉ fourth day of yᵉ third month, (May) in yᵉ Second year of yᵉ reign of our Sovereign Lady Anne of England, &c., Queen, Annoque Domini, 1703.

JOHN GUEST,   CALEB PUSLY,
SAMUEL CARPENTER,   JOHN BLUNSTON,
SAMUEL FINNEY,   T   STORY, (another name nearly worn off.)

By Order of yᵉ President and Council,

JAMES LOGAN, Secretary   EDWARD SHIPPEN, President.

---

2. A Proclamation by Lieut. Governor Evans for defence against France and Spain

THE GREAT
SEAL OF
PENNSYLVANIA.

By the honorable John Evans, Esq , with her Majesty's Royal Approbation, Lieutenant Governor of the Province of Pensilvania and Counties annexed.

A PROCLAMATION

FORASMUCH as The Queen's most Exellent Majestie and the Rest of her Majestie's Allies are now Engaged in a Vigorous Warr against France and Spain, for Maintaining and Preserving the Liberty and Ballance of Europe, which as it Engages the Subjects of the said Crowns and States in open hostilitie. So it laies her Majestie's Subjects in this Government under a Necessity of being well armed and disciplined, as well for the honour and service of her Majestie as for the Defence and Preservation of our Religion, Lives, and Liberties, all which her Majesty having duly weighed and Considered, was Graciously pleased to Command that due preparation should be made in this Government tor the Defence and Security of the same, against any attempt that might be made upon it by the Enemy during this time of Warr   THEREFORE, in Obedience to her Majesty's Royal Commands, and to the End that the Inhabitants of the said Counties might be in a Posture of Defence and Readiness to withstand and Repell all Acts of hostilitie that the Enemy shall attempt against them, I doe hereby strictly Command and Require all Persons residing in the said Counties, that forthwith they Doe Provide themselves with a Good firelock and Ammunition in Order to Inlist themselves in the Militia which I now am setting in this Government, and Every Inhabitant thereof as aforesaid shall without delay Repair unto and Inlist himself with the Officer or Officers Commissioned to Command in that District where such Inhabitant dwells. And I Doe further Command all Persons that they take due notice hereof and give obedience, and be to their utmost aiding and assisting to the said Officers in all things relating to the Exercising the Power Given them in their Commissions, as they will answer the Contrary at their Peril. Given under my hand and Great Seal at Philadelphia, the six and twentieth day of May. in the third year of the Reign of Our Sovereign Lady Queen Anne over England, &c., Annoq° Domini, 1704.

GOD SAVE THE QUEEN.

JOHN EVANS.

—

3. A Proclamation by Lieutenant Governor Evans against Immorality and Profaneness

By the Honourable Colloneil John Evans, Lieutenant Governor of the Province of Pennsylvania and Counties annexed

A PROCLAMATION,

Against Immorality and Profaneness

WHEREAS, it hath Pleased Almighty God from the Treasures of his Infinite Goodness to extend his favours in an Eminent degree, and pour down His peculiar Blessings upon this Colony, from the first Erecting thereof, as well by Bestowing a happy Success on the Endeavours of its Inhabitants, and crowning what so lately was a Wilderness with a large affluence of all the Necessaries and Comforts of life, as by supporting it in an undisturbed Peace and Tranquility during all the Commotions that have deeply afflicted other parts of the Christian World, and Continuing to us the Enjoyment of those Manifold Mercies, which rightly used tend to make a people truly happy. All which divine Bounties as they loudly call for the most humble and hearty Acknowledgments, so they ought more deeply to Impress a just sense of the Great obligations upon us, so to regulate our Lives, with Care and Circumspection, in a true Obedience and Conformity to God's holy Laws, that we may not, Instead of making grateful Returns, by Impiety or Negligence provoke the just rage of the ALMIGHTY to withdraw his divine Protection, and inflict on Us the severe Chastisement of his Just displeasure.

Notwithstanding all which I cannot but be sensible that too Many forgetting all those obligations, that as persons professing the Holy Christian Religion they indispensably lye Under, have given themselves a Loose in their Lives and Conversations, and manifestly trampled on their Positively known Duties in many Vicious Practices and Immoralities, to the great offence of ALMIGHTY GOD, in the breach of his Divine Laws,

62

as well as of our Civil Institutions, and to the scandal of sober Men and great discredit of this Government, Which Practices, if not timely prevented, may terminate in an Utter Depravation of manners, through the Encouragement taken from those fatal and pernicious Examples, by persons whose better Education and Inclinations might otherwise have restrained them within the Bounds of Sobriety and Virtue; but from those many Instances sett before their Eyes, are in danger of being hurried on not only to their own Ruin, but of becoming accessary to the Incensing and drawing down upon Us the Vengeance of Heaven.

In a deep Consideration of which, and to the end that all possible Discouragements may be given to the Growth of these Enormities, I have, through a sense of the duty I owe to God and ye Care of the People committed to my charge, By and with the advice and Consent of the Council of this Province and Territories, thought fit to Publish and Declare, that I will Discountenance and severely Punish all manner of Vice, Immorality and Profaneness in all persons whatsoever within this Government, that shall be guilty of the same And I doe hereby strictly forbid all manner of Debauchery, Lewdness, Drunkenness, profane Swearing, Cursing, Rioting, breaking of the Sabbath, Night walking at unreasonable hours without Lawful Business, and all other Disorders whatsoever that are contrary to the Duties of a Christian Life and the Rules of true Virtue. And I doe strictly Command and Require all Magistrates, Justices, Sheriffs, Constables, and all Officers whatsoever, and others her Majesties good Subjects, that they not only be regular and Circumspect in their own lives, that, by their good Examples, they may incite those that behold them to the Practice of Virtue, but also that they be very Diligent in the Discovery and effectual Prosecution of all offenders, and that they rigorously putt in Execution all the good and wholesome Laws and Ordinances provided against the aforesaid and such other Immoralities, without favor, partiality, or Affection to any person whatsoever, as they will answer it to Almighty God and incur my utmost displeasure And for the more effectual publication hereof, I doe require and Command the Justices of Quarter Sessions at their respective County Courts in this Government, and the Mayor and Recorder of the City of Philadelphia, that they cause this my proclamation to be publicly read in open Court immediately after their charge is given to the Grand Jury. Also that the Ministers of the Churches and Several Congregations within this Province and Territories, Cause the same to be Read in the time of Divine Service, at their respective places of Worship, at least six times in every year. And that they be very diligent in Discouraging all manner of Vice and Immorality in their Auditors, in Exhorting them to the exercise of Piety and Virtue Given at Philadelphia the Ninth day of October, in the third year of the Reign of our Sovereign Lady Anne, by the Grace of God of England, Scotland, France and Ireland, Queen, Defender of the Faith, &c, and the twenty-fourth of the Proprietaries Government, Annoque Domini, 1704.

GOD SAVE THE QUEEN

JOHN EVANS

4   A Proclamation for a Thanksgiving for the Victories over the French.

[This Proclamation has been much mutilated]

THE GREAT
SEAL OF
PENNSYLVANIA

By the Honorable Collonel John Evans, Lieutenant Governor of the Province of Pennsylvania, and Counties of New Castle, Kent, and Sussex, in Delaware.

WHEREAS, The Queen's most Excellent Majesty by her Royal Proclamation given at her Court at K**** the one and twentieth day of May last, most devoutly and thankfully acknowledging the * * * * Almighty God in Continuing to her Majesty his Protection and Assistance in * * * * and For Disappointing the Boundless ambition of Fr * * * Majesty, is now engaged, and in Conjunction with those of her Allies under the Command of His Grace John Duke of Ma * * * *, General of Her Majesty's Land Forces, a Signal and Glorious Victory in Brabant over the French Armies * * * *, restoring the greatest part of the Spanish Netherlands to ye Posssession of the House of Austria, in the person of * * * the third, by the Happy and wonderful progress of the Confederate Forces, and also in Blessing the Arms of Her Majesty and those of Her Allies with Great Success in Catalonia and other parts of Spain, Was Graciously pleased in Consideration, that such Great and Public Blessings doe call for Public and Solemn Acknowledgments, to Appoint and Command, with the Advice of Her Majesty's Privy Council, that a General Thanksgiving to Almighty God for these Mercies should be observed in her Dominions. AND WHEREAS, I have received Directions together with the said Proclamation, from the Right Honorable the Lord Commissioners of Trade and Plantations, that in conformity to Her Majesty's Royal Pleasure in Her other Dominions, I should also appoint in this Her Majesty's Province, a Proper and Special day for a Solemn Thanksgiving to Almighty God for the mercies aforesaid. I have therefore, in obedience thereto, thought fit to Appoint and Command that on the sixteenth day of January next ensuing, a Solemn General Publick Thanksgiving be observed by all her Majesty's Loving Subjects within this her Majesty's Province and in the Counties aforesaid   On which Day all Persons are Required to Refrain from their usual Labour and Employment and Repair to Divine * * in the Publick Places of Worship, Devoutly to return to Almighty God, the Author of all Blessings, most humble and hearty Thanks and Acknowledgments For his aforesaid mercies * * they tender the Favour of Heaven upon pain of being Punished * * * mners of Her Majesty's Royal Commands in the Pe * * * Religious and Necessary * * * *   Witness my Hand and the Great Seal of the Government at Philadelphia, * * * * * * * Year of the Reign of our Sovereign Lady Anne of England, Scotland, France and Ireland, Queen, Defender of the Faith, &c. Annoq⁰ Domini 1760.

GOD SAVE THE QUEEN.

JOHN EVANS.

—

VIII —*Letter from Mr. Andrew Banks of Juniata County, on the Early History of that County*

[This Letter was received in reply to the Circular issued by the Society a few years since. In the fourth volume, part second, of the Memoirs of the Society, published last year, the Circular and several of the replies to it may be found.]

About the year 1758 Capt James Patterson settled on the Juniata river on the spot where Mexico now stands, his object appears to have been to trade with the Indians for their lands ; he obtained from them all their lands lying north from that place for the distance of three or four miles lying on Doe run ; the original title of all those lands was vested in him. Although a trader he, as it appeared, did not rely upon the peaceful habits of those he traded with, for in order to keep them in awe he converted an oak log into a cannon and discharged it frequently in their hearing, which greatly intimidated them. On a certain occasion when the men were absent from the rude station, the barking of a dog drew Mrs Patterson's attention, when to her great surprise she discovered a large group of Indians making their way towards her. She at once stationed herself beside the mimic cannon, menacing defiance, calling aloud " Come on you yellow dogs you," whereupon the whole batch disappeared under covert of the thicket.

About the year 1760 and subsequently, came a number of individuals, principally Irish or their descendants, from York and Adams counties, but principally from Cumberland county along the waters of the Conedoguinet. They were generally persons about to set out into the world, their families were mostly small, and generally in low circumstances. About the period above alluded to William Maclay, late of Harrisburg, settled on the Juniata, where Mifflintown, the seat of justice of Juniata county now stands, the house that he occupied is yet in a good state of preservation, and about the same period Robert Nelson settled on the " Cedarspring ;" the old mansion is yet standing, a part of the other cotemporary settlers were James Purdy, William Henderson, James Gibson, William Sharon, Hugh Sharon, Alexander Armstrong, Hugh McAlister, James Dickey, Nathaniel Dickey, Samuel Mitchel, Samuel Sharon, and others.

Mifflintown was first improved as a town about the year 1786. Its improvement was very slow until the county was disannexed from Mifflin in 1829, since which time some valuable improvements have been made. Besides the necessary public buildings, two brick churches, one Presby terian, the other Lutheran, have been erected, and an iron foundry and other valuable improvements were made in 1844.

Mrs Charlotte Thompson of Delaware township in this county, who is grand daughter to Capt. James Patterson above alluded to, informs that she has in her possession a large number of papers which belonged to her grandfather, among which are a number of letters in correspondence between him and other officers in the army of General Forbes in 1758, and during the French war at various periods These documents are said to contain much valuable information ; copies can be had on application.   In 1773, when the writer first visited this country, the improvements generally were a small hut or cabin house, and barn of like description, with a few acres of cleared land. Improvements progressed very slowly until about the beginning of the present century, when a number of German emigrants from Lancaster, Berks, Montgomery, Chester, and other eastern counties, bought out a large number of the original inhabitants, and from that time the county began rapidly to improve The improvements now generally are a frame, stone, or brick dwelling house, a stone or frame bank barn, and other necessary buildings in proportion ; and the lands are all cleared with the exception of hill lands for timber and fuel

Seventy years ago, and many years subsequent, wild game were very plenty in our forests. It consisted of deer, bear, wolf, some panthers, wild cat, otter, raccoon, squirrel, rabbit, and beaver The fowl were turkey, pheasant, pigeon, partridge, &c Game of almost every kind gradually disappeared, the writer has not known of deer's being caught for the last nine or ten years, and the same may be said of every other species of game, with the exception of the red fox, who fully maintains his ground. It has been an ancient observation that the red fox extirpated the grey, and such appears to be the fact.

The first emigrants found this county an unbroken forest, in the midst of which they settled, exposed to numerous privations, as no supplies could be had nearer than their native places, and when they did furnish supplies from their industry, they had to take it over the mountains from thirty to forty miles to get it ground.

I do not know of any person who have made any historical collection either ancient or modern

The inhabitants of this part of the state are, and have been an agricultural people, whose attentions were not drawn to these objects.

The early court records of this county were deposited in Carlisle up till the year 1789, when what is now Juniata, Mifflin, and Centre counties were disannexed from Cumberland and denominated Mifflin County ; consequently the early court records are to be found at Carlisle and Lewistown.

I have no knowledge of any state or county maps further than such as are contained in our Geography.

Do not know of any metals or ancient coins ; have not seen any of the Continental money for many years.

I have no ancient documents of historical interest.

I have no drawings either public or private.

66

I have not any documents as those mentioned.
Such documents are not to be expected from a private citizen.
The Universities of Penn. are matter of history.

Mifflintown, the capital of Juniata county, was laid out into lots and began to be improved, as a town, about the year 1786, was incorporated immediately after the county was organized, in 1830. Thompsontown had a few years later origin, and Mexico still later, but the Postmasters of these places are more competent to identify their true origin.

The township of "Fermanagh" in its original dimensions contained what is now denominated "Walker" township, lying on the south side of what is now designated "Fermanagh," and also "Fayette," lying N. E. Its present dimensions are four miles square.

With respect to population generally, it has become a matter of history by the late census, and in regard to births, longevity and deaths, having never kept any record beyond the limits of my own family, the writer can exhibit nothing specific. There was, however, a gentleman by the name of James Butler, Esq., many years a citizen of this county, who kept a record of all the births and deaths, which fell under his notice, until his death which happened about two years ago at the age of 87 years. His papers would be a good acquisition, they can be obtained (or at least, copies) by applying to James Matthew, Esq., Mifflintown.

The first epidemic which prevailed in this country was in the year 1763, it was a nervous fever and very mortal; it was more general along the Juniata river, but it also extended widely over the interior of the country. The next that prevailed, commenced in 1803, in the month of August. It was awfully mortal, a bilious fever, the author knew an instance in the small village of Mifflintown, of four deaths in the course of one evening, two of them in one house; it prevailed with great malignity for two successive years, after that it became milder. The next epidemic which prevailed was a Typhus fever, it commenced in December, 1812, it raged unabated till about the month of June, 1813, when it subsided by degrees. All the different grades of constitution yielded equally before it. A few hours, or at most a few days, three or four days at most, brought on a crisis, the more robust the patient, it appeared the more fatal. It appeared to be most fatal in winter. The summer heats commence generally about the middle of June, and continue till the last of August, the latter is generally the warmest month, the thermometer rising to 86, 90, and sometimes even 95 degrees of Farhenheit. Winter commences about the last of December and continues till the middle of February. The country is made up of alternate ranges of hill and valley; in the flat lands limestone prevails, and in the higher a gravel, the agriculturists begin to reckon the latter soil the best as being more certain when duly attended to. The products are those of the other parts of Pennsylvania, viz.—wheat, rye, corn, oats, buckwheat, some barley, with potatoes and other vegetables. The general employment of the inhabitants is agriculture, which is well attended to, the various mechanic arts recieve their due attention. The merchants generally pursue their business with much industry and regularity, and all the different classes, when duly attending their pursuits seldom fail of a competency

No Biographical notices have fallen under my notice other than those contained in history.

I have not any knowledge of such tables as those asked for.

We have no public library.

The first newspaper established in this county was edited by Michael Duffey, in Mifflintown, about the year 1794, it was discontinued in a year or two, and two others have been established. The " Mifflin Eagle" was published by B N. Gallaher a series of years, and afterwards by Sam'l G. Nesbit, but now discontinued, and five years since the " Spirit of the Times" was established by Samuel Sheack, and and edited by James G. Sample.

The only original author either of prose or poetry which this county has at any time produced, was James Butler, Esq., already noticed, who used to indulge himself in framing a kind of doggerel verses, mostly satirical, notwithstanding which, they possessed some degree of merit, some of his pieces were published, one in particular on the subject of St. Clair's defeat, which of course was tragical. It possessed considerable merit, and was published, but not now in circulation as far as known. He also wrote and published a novel entitled "Fortune's Foot-Ball," which possessed some merit ; by having recourse to his papers, manuscripts, &c , they no doubt can be procured.

No history of any of our towns or townships, or of our county, has been published, or materials collected for such purpose as far as known.

About the year 1762, the inhabitants undertook to build a church for the Presbyterian denomination. They raised it one story, when they were driven away by the Indians. Four years elapsed before their return ; they then found it damaged, and threw it down and erected one on a larger scale. It was built near the Cedarspring and denominated the " Cedarspring church." It is now in ruins. In the year 1773, at the earliest period known to the writer, a Mr Kennedy officiated as stated pastor; they had erected a dwelling house near the church, and in which he lived. On some misunderstanding's taking place, he did not stay long, and about the year 1777, the congregation prepared a call for a Mr. Hugh Magill, and he accepted. He continued his labors till about the year 1797 ; being worn down by age, he declined. A call was then prepared for Mr. Matthew Brown, who began his ministry in the year 1801, and continued three years and left. In 1804 a call was accepted by Rev. John Hutchison who continued to officiate 39 years ; he died the 10th day of November last.

The congregation being large, for the sake of convenience a separation was made and two churches erected, one at Mifflintown and the other near Mc'Allistersville ; a charter was obtained by the style of the " Presbyterian Congregation of Cedarspring, composing the Congregations of Mifflin and Lost Creek " and so it remains. A congregation of " The associate reformed " Presbyterians have existed here since about the year 1775, when William Logan became its Pastor. They erected a church, which is still in good preservation, about the year 1794, having previous nothing but a tent to assemble at. It is still a respectable congregation under the Pastoral Charge of a Mr. Shields. Not aware of any inscriptions either on or about any of the churches other than the ordinary monumental notices.

Have no knowledge of the dockets in the offices at the seat of Justice. A professor of the law will be best able to satisfy in that case

The same answer

There were three mounds known to the writer at the early history of this country. One at the junction of the Aughwick creek and the Juniata river near the town of Newton hamilton, in Mifflin county, one at the junction of the Kishicoquillas, at or near Lewistown in the same county ; and one at the junction of the Cocolamaus near Millerstown, in Perry county The tradition of the country is, that a war existed between the Delawares and the Tuscaroras, that a pitched battle ensued at the former place, at which the latter tribe was defeated, when they retired down the river to the mouth of the Kishicoquillas, and there made a second stand, and were again defeated. They retired again to the latter place, made a third stand, and were a third time defeated, which last conflict so much weakened the Tuscaroras that the nation became extinct, not being afterwards able to raise any more warriors There is not any person now living here who was contemporary with the Indians Have not any knowledge of Indian relics in this place The writer has read many conjectures relative to their origin Such as their being sprung from the ancient Hebrews, on account of their proneness to offer sacrifices to their deities, in which there is much similarity, together with the structure of the language of some of the tribes. Some historians have been convinced of the fact, but still it is vague conjecture after all that has been said . with respect to the Indian names of rivers, mountains &c., those names have all some peculiar meaning in the Indian dialect, for instance, the Alleghany, Ohio, and Mississippi, all mean the same thing in three different dialects, and signifies *white water*.

There are not any soldiers of the revolution now living in this neighbourhood. The writer of this article recollects it distinctly. The subject of the revolution is matter of history, and has been generally read ; the inhabitants of this county were all *Whigs*, and the writer well remembers the fearful forbodings which took possession of many of our most staunch whigs on the receipt of some unfavorable news The first troops that marched from here were those who joined the army of General Montgomery, destined for Quebec. The writer had a first cousin on that expedition, belonging to the company of the brave *Hendricks*, who fell at the head of his company fighting at "The barriers ; " but the fate of those worthy men is well known in the history of our country.* The next troops that marched were two companies of volunteers, each company containing 80 men besides their officers ; the one commanded by Captain Gibson, the other by Captain Purdy. They repaired to the camp in the beginning of the year 1776, and performed a tour of two months, afterwards the troops marched agreeably to their draught, which order was continued. The writer also well recollects the enthusi-

* See the narrative of John Joseph Henry, of the expedition against Quebec.

astic joy manifested on the capture of Cornwallis, and the patriotic songs of those days are still familiar

No doubt need be entertained that the documents alluded to in the foregoing, can be had, (copies at least) if not the original.

A SONG OF THE REVOLUTION ON THE EVENT OF A VICTORY.

Hark! Hark! The joyful news that's come,
Sound, sound the trumpet beat the drum,
            Let manly joys abound
Let Freedom's sacred ensigns wave,
Supported by the virtuous brave,
            Our victory is crowned.

From East to West from South to North
The brave American sons stood forth,
            All terrible in arms
Their rights, their freedom to maintain,
Undaunted tread the bloody plain,
            And smile at war's alarms

Montgomery claims our just applause,
He to assert fair freedom's cause
            Domestic peace forsook,
The sword he grasped and boldly on,
Till ebbing life was fairly gone,
            His valor never shook.

Kind Providence our troops inspires
With more than Greek and Roman fires,
            Therefore our cause prevails;
Preserved by Heaven, a virtuous few
Tyrannic legions shall subdue,
            For Justice seldom fails.

Let brimful bumpers flow around,
And songs to their just praise resound,
            Who have their bravery shown.
To Mercer and Montgomery,
To Mifflin, Gates, and Green so free,
            And Glorious Washington.

Thus I have very imperfectly sketched a few of the reminiscences of this country, agreeably to the questions proposed, hoping that it may not be altogether uninteresting, however imperfectly executed. They are some few of the results of my observation during a period of 72 years; all which is respectfully submitted.

ANDREW BANKS.

Fermanagh township, Juniata County, Penn'a.

IX.—*A Sermon preached on the eve of the Battle of Brandywine (September 10, 1777,) by the Rev. Joab Trout, to a large portion of the American Army.*

(Communicated by Mr. John H. Lick of Fredericksburg, Lebanon County.)

"They that take the sword shall perish by the sword."

Soldiers and Countrymen,—We have met this evening, perhaps for the last time. We have shared the toil of march, the peril of fight, and the dismay of the retreat, alike we have endured the cold and hunger, the contumely of the internal foe and the courage of foreign oppression. We have sat, night after night, beside the camp-fire, we have together heard the roll of the reveille which called us to duty, or the beat of the tattoo which gave the signal for the hardy sleep of the soldier with the earth for his bed and knapsack for his pillow.

And now, soldiers and brethren, we have met in the peaceful valley on the eve of battle, while the sunlight is dying away behind yonder heights, the sunlight that, to morrow morn, will glimmer on scenes of blood. We have met amid the whitening tents of our encampment, in time of terror and gloom, have gathered together, God grant it may not be the last time.

It is a solemn moment. Brethren, does not the voice of nature seem to echo the sympathies of the hour? The flag of our country droops heavily from yonder staff; the breeze has died away along the green plains of Chadd's Ford—the heights of the Brandywine arise gloomily beyond yonder stream—all nature pauses in solemn silence, on the eve of to-morrow.

"They that take the sword shall perish by the sword." And have they not taken the sword?

Let the desolated plain, the blood-trodden valley, the burned farmhouse, the sacked village and the ravaged town, answer—let the whitening bones of the farmer strown along the fields of his homestead answer—let the starving mother with her babe clinging to the withered breast that can afford no sustenance—let her answer with the death-rattle ringing with the murmuring tones that mark the last struggle of life—let the dying mother and her babe answer. It was but a day past and our land slept in the quiet of peace. War was not here—wrong was not here. Fraud and war, misery and want dwelt not among us. From the eternal solitude of the green woods, arose the smoke of the settler's cabins, golden fields of corn looked forth from amid the waste of the wilderness and the glad music of human voices awoke the silence of the forest.

Now, behold the change. Under the shadow of a pretext, under the sanctity of the name of God, invoking the Redeemer to their aid, these foreign hirelings slay our people. They throng our towns, they darken our plains, and now encompass our post on the lovely plain of Chadd's Ford.

"They that take the sword shall perish by the sword." Brethren' think me not unworthy of belief when I tell you the doom of the British is near, when I tell you that beyond the cloud that now enshrouds us, I see gathering, thick and fast, the darker cloud and the blacker storm of Divine retribution. They may conquer us to-morrow; might and wrong may prevail, and we may be driven from this field—but the hour of God's own vengeance will come.

Aye, if in the vast solitudes of eternal space, if in the heart of the boundless universe, there throbs the being of an awful God, quick to avenge and sure to punish guilt, then will George of Brunswick feel the vengeance of the eternal Jehovah. A blight will be upon his life, a blight will be upon his children and upon his people. Great God, how dread the punishment! A crowded populace, peopling the dense towns where the man of money thrives, while the laborer starves, want striding among the people in all its forms of terror; an ignorant and God-defying priesthood chuckling over the miseries of millions, a proud and merciless nobility adding wrong to wrong and heaping insult upon robbery and fraud, crime and want linked hand in hand and tempting men to deeds of woe and death—these are a part of the doom and retribution that come upon the English throne and the English people.

Soldiers, I look around upon your familiar faces with a strange interest. To morrow morning we will all go forth to battle, for I need not tell you that your unworthy minister will march with you, invoking God's aid in the fight—we will march forth to battle! Need I exhort you to fight the good fight, to fight for your homesteads, for your wives and children? I might urge you by the galling memories of British wrong, I might paint all this again in the vivid colors of the terrible reality, if I thought your courage needed such wild excitement. But I know you are strong in the might of the Lord. You will march forth to battle on the morrow with light hearts and determined spirits, though the duty of avenging the dead may rest heavy on your souls.

And in the hour of battle, when all around is lit by the lurid cannon-glare, and the piercing musket-flash, when the wounded strew the ground and the dead litter your path, then remember that God is with you, God the awful and infinite fights for you and will triumph.

You have taken the sword, but not in the spirit of wrong and ravage. You have taken the sword for your homes, your wives, your little ones; for truth, for justice and right, and to you the promise is. Be of good cheer, your foes have taken the sword in defiance of all that man holds dear, they shall perish by the sword.

And now farewell! Many of us may fall to morrow: God rest the souls of the fallen! Many of us may live to tell the story, and in the memory of all will ever linger the quiet scene of this autumnal night.

Solemn twilight advances over the valley, the woods of the opposite heights fling their long shadows over the green of the meadow, around us are the tents of the Continental host, the suppressed bustle of the camp, the hurried tramp of the soldiers too and fro among the tents, the stillness and awe that mark the eve of the battle.

When we meet again, may the shadows of twilight be flung over a peaceful land God in heaven grant it.

Let us pray:

A PRAYER.

Great Father, we bow before thee, we invoke thy blessing, we deprecate thy wrath, we return thee thanks for the past, we ask thy aid for the furure; for we are in times of trouble, O Lord, and sore beset by foes, merciless and unpitying. The sword gleams over our land, the dust of the sod is dampened with the blood of our neighbors and friends. O God of mercy, we pray thy blessing on the American arms. Make the man of our hearts strong in thy wisdom; bless, we beseech thee, with renewed life and strength, our hope and thy instrument, even George Washington. Shower thy counsels on the Honourable the Continental Congress. Visit the tents of our host, comfort the soldier in his wounds and afflictions, nerve him for the fight and prepare him for the hour of death

And in the hour of defeat, O God of hosts, do thou be our stay, and in the hour of triumph be thou our guide. Teach us to be merciful. Though the memory of galling wrongs be at our hearts knocking for admittance, that they may fill us with the desire of revenge, yet let us, O Lord, spare the vanquished, though they never spared us In the hour of death do thou guide us to the abode prepared for the blest. So shall we return thanks to thee through Christ our Redeemer. GOD PROSPER THE CAUSE. Amen.